HANNAH,

IT'S BEEN FUN GETTING TO KNOW YOU OVER THE LAST FEW MONTHS!

I HOPE YOU ENJOY THE BOOK. :)

JON STATOS

J. STATOS

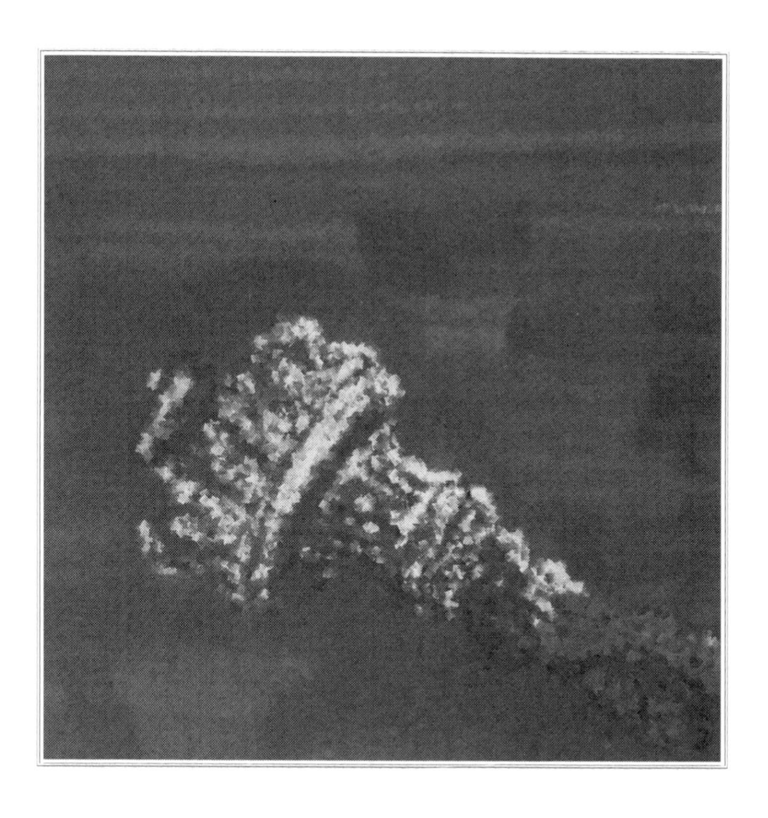

"When I say unto the wicked, Thou shalt surely die; and thou givest him not warning, nor speakest to warn the wicked from his wicked way, to save his life; the same wicked man shall die in his iniquity; but his blood will I require at thine hand."

- Ezekiel 3:15

Dedication

I dedicate this book to my country
and birthplace, America,

and to those who live within her.

I hope that those virtues
which made America great
will not perish from the
earth.

How America Ends

Written by

J. David States

Bible quotations from the King James Version.

Published via Kindle Direct Publishing

ISBN: 9781077313064

Table of Contents

Foreward

~

Dear Reader,

Let me first say that I am no prophet or fortuneteller; I am simply an ordinary man living in extraordinary times, who possesses a keen interest in the direction that human history will take. I procrastinated writing this book because such "dire prognostications" are hardly a rarity in these times, and I myself tend to look upon predictions of future events with great skepticism. But the fact remains that God in His revealed Word, the Bible, has left us certain truths, and truth is important; acting upon it can bring great blessing, and ignoring it can bring great detriment. Upon studying for myself the Biblical prophecies which are outlined in this book, and upon seeing their culmination growing ever nearer in current events around me, I became convinced that certain predetermined things will soon transpire. Having this certainty of conviction in my own mind, I cannot in good conscience sit quietly in a corner, knowing that my homeland will one day burn.

I do not know the future; absolute knowledge of things yet to come is something that God Almighty has reserved for Himself alone. In His mercy, however,

He sometimes forewarns His people of coming destructions and judgments. In this book I will simply present what God has already asserted in His Word; it is for you, Reader, to decide what to do for yourself upon hearing these things. This book will not be easy to read, and it has not been easy to write. A great many fears have needed to be overcome in order to write it: fear of the message itself, fear of the implications of that message, fear of how that message will be received.

I can only say that these things are certain to me because God has said them, and the flow of current events (to my mind) seems to be converging towards an eventual culmination. (Such was my conviction that I wrote, edited, and published this book in less than three weeks.) I encourage you to please read this work carefully and with an open mind. Consider what you have seen in your life, and what God has clearly spoken in His Word. Strive to see truth without fear, trusting that ultimately all events unfold as our Almighty God permits.

May God bless you, your family, and America's remaining time.

J. David States
Summer 2019

Chapter 1:
America's Dominance Will End

Daniel 2 and 7

~

"Now I Nebuchadnezzar praise and extol and honour the King of heaven, all whose works are truth, and his ways judgment: and those that walk in pride he is able to abase."

Daniel 4:37

The Prophecies of Daniel 2

Long before humanity was given the completed Bible, God spoke to kings, emperors, and peoples through His chosen prophets, who conveyed God's messages to the appropriate recipients and who then recorded those messages for posterity. These divine messages were often portents of future events or warnings of future judgment. Daniel was one such prophet, and the Biblical book of Daniel (chapter 2) records God's message to the ancient king Nebuchadnezzar of Babylon (probably Nebuchadnezzar II of the Neo-Babylonian Empire).

The second chapter of Daniel tells us that in the second year of Nebuchadnezzar's reign, this king of Babylon was visited in the night by a troubling dream which distressed him so much that he could not sleep. Nebuchadnezzar summoned all the greatest scientists of his day, the magicians, astrologers, sorcerers, and "Chaldeans" of Babylon, and demanded that they should reveal to him what the dream meant, or be destroyed:

"And in the second year of the reign of Nebuchadnezzar Nebuchadnezzar dreamed dreams, wherewith his spirit was troubled, and his sleep brake from him.

Then the king commanded to call the magicians, and the astrologers, and the sorcerers, and the Chaldeans, for to shew the king his dreams. So they came and stood before the king.

And the king said unto them, I have dreamed a dream, and my spirit was troubled to know the dream.

Then spake the Chaldeans to the king in Syriack, O king, live for ever: tell thy servants the dream, and we will shew the interpretation.

The king answered and said to the Chaldeans, The thing is gone from me: if ye will not make known unto me the dream, with the interpretation thereof, ye shall be cut in pieces, and your houses shall be made a dunghill."

Daniel 2:1-5

The dream had made a deep impression upon Nebuchadnezzar, and the king simply was not in the mood for the usual obsequious smoke-and-mirrors tricks that the politically-minded "wise men" of the time often employed. Nebuchadnezzar wanted the undiluted truth, and if his science ministers could not deliver the answers he required, they were useless to him... and expendable.

Providentially, the young man Daniel and several of his friends had been placed amongst the advisors of the king's court. Daniel was a Hebrew slave, taken to Babylon after the siege and capture of Jerusalem by the Babylonian armies. The first chapter of Daniel recounts how Daniel and his three friends Hananiah, Mishael, and Azariah were selected to serve before the king as the most worthy of the Hebrew captives.

Nebuchadnezzar had issued a kill order upon all the wise men of Babylon if they were unable to provide the interpretation of his dream, and this order was given to Arioch, the captain of the king's guard. Daniel and the other captives serving as junior advisors in the king's court were also subject to this kill order, but Daniel was well liked by Arioch and the captain was able to gain Daniel an audience before Nebuchadnezzar. After receiving an unspecified time extension from Nebuchadnezzar, Daniel and his friends prayed to God and Daniel received the interpretation of the king's dream in a night vision:

"Thou, O king, sawest, and behold a great image. This great image, whose brightness was excellent, stood

before thee; and the form thereof was terrible.

This image's head was of fine gold, his breast and his arms of silver, his belly and his thighs of brass,

His legs of iron, his feet part of iron and part of clay.

Thou sawest till that a stone was cut out without hands, which smote the image upon his feet that were of iron and clay, and brake them to pieces.

Then was the iron, the clay, the brass, the silver, and the gold, broken to pieces together, and became like the chaff of the summer threshingfloors; and the wind carried them away, that no place was found for them: and the stone that smote the image became a great mountain, and filled the whole earth.

This is the dream; and we will tell the interpretation thereof before the king.

Thou, O king, art a king of kings: for the God of heaven hath given thee a kingdom, power, and strength, and glory.

And wheresoever the children of men dwell, the beasts of the field and the fowls of the heaven hath he given into thine hand, and hath made thee ruler over them all. Thou art this head of gold.

And after thee shall arise another kingdom inferior to thee, and another third kingdom of brass, which shall bear rule over all the earth.

And the fourth kingdom shall be strong as iron: forasmuch as iron breaketh in pieces and subdueth all things: and as iron that breaketh all these, shall it break in pieces and bruise.

And whereas thou sawest the feet and toes, part of

potters' clay, and part of iron, the kingdom shall be divided; but there shall be in it of the strength of the iron, forasmuch as thou sawest the iron mixed with miry clay.

And as the toes of the feet were part of iron, and part of clay, so the kingdom shall be partly strong, and partly broken.

And whereas thou sawest iron mixed with miry clay, they shall mingle themselves with the seed of men: but they shall not cleave one to another, even as iron is not mixed with clay.

And in the days of these kings shall the God of heaven set up a kingdom, which shall never be destroyed: and the kingdom shall not be left to other people, but it shall break in pieces and consume all these kingdoms, and it shall stand for ever.

Forasmuch as thou sawest that the stone was cut out of the mountain without hands, and that it brake in pieces the iron, the brass, the clay, the silver, and the gold; the great God hath made known to the king what shall come to pass hereafter: and the dream is certain, and the interpretation thereof sure."

Daniel 2:31-45

The message given to Nebuchadnezzar was of great significance, not only to the king himself, but to all future generations of humanity thereafter. Nebuchadnezzar's great unease was put to rest; the dream seemed to guarantee the dominance of Babylon over other nations for the duration of Nebuchadnezzar's own reign, at least. I doubt that Nebuchadnezzar cared overmuch about those lesser kingdoms which would eventually succeed his own: the Medo-Persian (or Archaemenid) Empire, the Grecian Empire, and the Roman Empire.

But the true importance of this vision is the advent of the unhewn stone, Jesus Christ, and the establishment of the kingdom of God. We see in Nebuchadnezzar's dream a representation of Christ's birth during the Roman Empire's time of dominance, and the growth of the Christian faith like a "mountain filling the whole earth." The Stone dashes in pieces all kings and empires, representing the endurance of God's kingdom as nations of men rise and fall. Indeed Rome would attempt to eradicate the fledgling Christian faith, but that faith outlasted Rome, eventually becoming the official faith of the Roman Empire under Constantine and then the core of Western Civilization itself. And the faith of the Lord Jesus Christ endures today; God has promised that it will outlast all human civilizations and empires.

Why is Daniel 2 significant to us today? Firstly, this passage demonstrates several Biblical prophecies which history has proven to be true. The sequential rise and fall of these empires, the advent of Christ during the height of Rome's power, and the growth of the Christian church were all foretold by God long before these events actually occurred. Additionally, the Bible is explicit that God does not merely see all human outcomes, but He also *ordains* and *orchestrates* them; Jeremiah 28:14 tells us that the ascendency of Babylon was not accident or happenstance:

"For thus saith the Lord of hosts, the God of Israel; I have put a yoke of iron upon the neck of all these nations, that they may serve Nebuchadnezzar king of Babylon; and they shall serve him: and I have given him the beasts of the field also."

Jeremiah 28:14

Finally, we see that Daniel was a true prophet of God and his words were true, and God's other prophecies given to Daniel which are currently unfulfilled are just as certain as those which have already come to pass. In a moment we will look at more of God's prophecies contained in Daniel 7, which have tremendous relevance for all those who are living within the United States of America today.

Daniel 7 and the Last Four Human Empires

In Daniel chapter 7, the prophet Daniel records a troubling night vision which he had during the first year of the reign of king Belshazzar of Babylon:

"In the first year of Belshazzar king of Babylon Daniel had a dream and visions of his head upon his bed: then he wrote the dream, and told the sum of the matters.

Daniel spake and said, I saw in my vision by night, and, behold, the four winds of the heaven strove upon the great sea.

And four great beasts came up from the sea, diverse one from another.

The first was like a lion, and had eagle's wings: I beheld till the wings thereof were plucked, and it was lifted up from the earth, and made stand upon the feet as a man, and a man's heart was given to it.

And behold another beast, a second, like to a bear, and it raised up itself on one side, and it had three ribs in the mouth of it between the teeth of it: and they said thus unto it, Arise, devour much flesh.

After this I beheld, and lo another, like a leopard, which had upon the back of it four wings of a fowl; the beast had also four heads; and dominion was given to it.

After this I saw in the night visions, and behold a fourth beast, dreadful and terrible, and strong exceedingly; and it had great iron teeth: it devoured and brake in pieces, and stamped the residue with the feet of it: and it was diverse from all the beasts that were before it; and it had ten horns.

I considered the horns, and, behold, there came up among them another little horn, before whom there were three of the first horns plucked up by the roots: and, behold, in this horn were eyes like the eyes of man, and a mouth speaking great things.

I beheld till the thrones were cast down, and the Ancient of days did sit, whose garment was white as snow, and the hair of his head like the pure wool: his throne was like the fiery flame, and his wheels as burning fire.

A fiery stream issued and came forth from before him: thousand thousands ministered unto him, and ten thousand times ten thousand stood before him: the judgment was set, and the books were opened.

I beheld then because of the voice of the great

words which the horn spake: I beheld even till the beast was slain, and his body destroyed, and given to the burning flame.

As concerning the rest of the beasts, they had their dominion taken away: yet their lives were prolonged for a season and time.

I saw in the night visions, and, behold, one like the Son of man came with the clouds of heaven, and came to the Ancient of days, and they brought him near before him.

And there was given him dominion, and glory, and a kingdom, that all people, nations, and languages, should serve him: his dominion is an everlasting dominion, which shall not pass away, and his kingdom that which shall not be destroyed.

I Daniel was grieved in my spirit in the midst of my body, and the visions of my head troubled me."

Daniel 7:1-15

In some ways, Daniel 7 is very similar to Daniel chapter 2, which we previously discussed. We see (similarly to Daniel 2) a succession of nations one after another, but this time represented by four different fierce beasts. After the four beast-kingdoms have their time of rule, God again makes an appearance. Some commentators, such as the esteemed Matthew Henry, have suggested that this passage of Scripture is simply a parallel passage to Daniel 2 and that it contains a duplicate message. Matthew Henry, in his commentaries, asserts that the lion with eagle's wings is the Chaldean monarchy of the Babylonian Empire, that the bear is therefore the Medo-Persian Empire, the leopard is the Greek Empire (Greciae), and the terrible beast is the Roman Empire. This is a conventional and traditional interpretation of this prophecy, but it is also demonstrably incorrect, as we will see.

There are significant and striking differences between the prophecies of Daniel 2 and Daniel 7. We see that Daniel 2 was intended as a message to a specific monarch, and that the message therein related to the intended recipient. In contrast, it cannot be demonstrated that Daniel 7 was likewise delivered to a specific king. Daniel saw the Daniel 7 prophecy in a night vision, and wrote down a summary of that vision. We know that Belshazzar was king of Babylon when Daniel had this dream, but it does not seem to be intended as a message to Belshazzar; in Daniel 5, Belshazzar was given a very different sign predicting a coup d'etet which would take Belshazzar's life the very night the message was delivered. Daniel 7 was intended for a different audience besides the Babylonian ruler of the day; it was intended for future end times believers.

We also know that the kingdoms of Daniel 7 are not Babylon, Medo-Persia, Greece, and Rome because Daniel 7 explicitly tells us so. Daniel, curious at the things he has been shown, as any of us would be, asks a bystander in the dream what these things might mean:

"I came near unto one of them that stood by, and asked him the truth of all this. So he told me, and made me know the interpretation of the things.

These great beasts, which are four, are four kings, which ***shall arise*** *out of the earth.*

But the saints of the most High shall take the kingdom, and possess the kingdom ***for ever*****,** *even* ***for ever and ever*****.***"*

Daniel 7:16-18

The answer to Daniel's question is quite clear: these are kingdoms which *shall arise* out of the earth, but they have not yet arisen. We can say something else about these kingdoms; they are the last four human empires. How can we know this with certainty? As in Daniel 2, after the end of the four beast-kingdoms, God makes an appearance, but this time it is not the initial advent (the Nativity) of Jesus Christ as in Daniel 2, but the triumphant return and coronation of Jesus Christ as the King of kings:

"I saw in the night visions, and, behold, one like the Son of man came with the clouds of heaven, and came to the Ancient of days, and they brought him near before him.

And there was given him dominion, and glory, and a kingdom, that all people, nations, and languages, should serve him: his dominion is an everlasting dominion, which shall not pass away, and his kingdom that which shall not be destroyed."

Daniel 7:13-14

"But the saints of the most High shall take the kingdom, and possess the kingdom for ever, even for ever and ever."

Daniel 7:18

Daniel 7:18 makes it perfectly clear; the coming of the Ancient of Days, the crowning of the Son of Man (Jesus Christ), and God's saints inheriting the kingdom of God are things that are promised at the end of human history (in the Biblical book of Revelation), which have not yet come to pass. The beast-nations of Daniel 7 are therefore the last four phases of human civilization before the culmination of history.

What does this mean for America today? The American Empire is today the world's *only* superpower, and America has held that position for nearly a century. The beast-kingdoms of Daniel 7 are likewise superpower-level nations; this is certain from Daniel 7:23 (speaking of the terrible beast-kingdom): "Thus he said, The fourth beast shall be the fourth kingdom upon earth, which shall be diverse from all kingdoms, and shall *devour the whole earth*, and shall *tread it down*, and *break it in pieces*."

Logically there are only two possible outcomes if the prophecies of Daniel 7 are indeed true. Either America is not one of the four beast-kingdoms, and therefore America will eventually be supplanted prior to the rise of these four kingdoms, or America *is* one of the four beast-kingdoms, and will one day be supplanted by the next kingdom which will follow it. Regardless of which path history takes, America will one day lose her dominance over the nations of the earth.

The Beast-Kingdoms and Their Identities

What then are the identities of these four beast-kingdoms? Do their roots and precursor nations already exist in the world today? Let us consider the beast-kingdoms of Daniel 7 again in greater detail:

- **The first beast was like a lion with eagles' wings.** The wings were removed from it, it was raised up above the earth, and it was made to stand up upon its feet like a man. A man's heart was given to it.
- **The second beast was like a bear.** It raised itself up on one side and it had three ribs in its jaws. It was told to "devour much flesh."
- **The third beast was like a leopard with four birds' wings on its back and four heads**; dominion was given to it.
- **The fourth beast was dreadful and terrible, exceedingly strong, with iron teeth and ten horns.** It devoured, broke in pieces, and trampled whatever was left with its feet. It was different from the other beasts; one of its horns supplants three others and

then makes war on God's saints.

Matthew Henry's mistaken indentity of the lion with eagles' wings as *ancient Babylon* is an undestandable conclusion; both the winged lion and the winged lion with the head and torso of a specific monarch (*lamassu*) are known emblems of royalty in many ancient near-east civilizations. His assessment may not have been too far off the mark though; for we see described by the apostle John in the book of Revelation a then-future kingdom which John termed "Mystery Babylon" -- so named because this future city and nation *resembled ancient Babylon* in wealth, prestige, and power, but its identity was unknown to John:

"And upon her forehead was a name written, MYSTERY, BABYLON THE GREAT, THE MOTHER OF HARLOTS AND ABOMINATIONS OF THE EARTH."
Revelation 17:5

In light of Jeremiah's prophecies concerning Babylon (which we will consider in later chapters), I am certain that The United States of America is both Mystery Babylon and the first beast, the winged lion. The lion has long been a heraldic symbol of Great Britain, America's mother country, and the eagles' wings, America, were eventually removed from Great Britain. Daniel 7 represents all of Anglo-American society, the pinnacle of Western civilization, together in this one beast, though obviously America is the preeminent power of this axis of nations. Many foreign nations' perception of America and Great Britain is that they are logical members of the same entity; in Hebrew "The United States of America" is ארצות הברית (artzote ha-*Brit*). Has any nation ever had a more *human* heart than the United States of America, with its core founding ideals of equality, liberty, and justice for all?

The second beast, the great and ravenous bear, is almost certainly an axis of powers with Russia at its core. Bible scholars more capable than myself have long associated the Gog (a ruler) and Magog (a nation) of Ezekiel 38 (as well as many Scriptural references to "the king of the north") with Russia. I will not dwell on this identification further, but if the topic interests you, Joel Rosenberg has written an excellent book on the subject of the Gog and Magog war of the Biblical book of Ezekiel. American President Ronald Reagan, a Christian, also believed that the Magog of the Bible was Soviet Russia. Russia has been represented as a great bear for centuries in political cartoons, satire, caricatures, and literature. Its association with the second beast of Daniel 7, especially in light of many other Biblical prophecies concerning the fall of Mystery Babylon, is self-evident and logical.

Some things, however, are too far removed from us and too obscure for us to be dogmatic about; such as the identity of the third beast, the leopard with four wings and four heads. I should mention that the word which the King James scholars rendered as "leopard" is a more generic Hebrew term; נמר (nemar) in modern Hebrew means "tiger." One of my Hebrew dictionaries specifically links the word with the Bengal tiger, *Panthera tigris tigris*. The inclusion of any type of large cat in the list of fierce carnivorous beasts depicted in Daniel 7 could be suitable. The national animal of India is the Bengal tiger, and I am personally inclined to think given that nation's current rapid modernization, huge population, and natural resources, India could be a reasonable choice for the third beast. China could be another viable candidate. Nothing drives conflict like the need to provide for a vast, hungry, growing population. But again, I must emphasize that I feel some of the things delineated in the Daniel 7 prophecy are beyond the scope of our shortsighted understanding of our times.

The fourth and terrible beast is almost too horrific for Daniel to describe, and he does so only with sparse details of some of its characteristics. This beast-kingdom has an aggressive need to dominate; what it cannot devour for itself, it destroys completely. This beast seems to be a coalition of nations, comprised of its horns; the little horn, which represents the Antichrist, seizes control and actively attempts to wipe out God's saints. The book of Revelation describes the rise of the Antichrist and his kingdom with more details; we can be quite certain of his identification with the little horn based upon his actions in Daniel 7 and Revelation 17:

- He will be charismatic and deceive the nations with great promises.
- He is associated with Satan and the pit of Hell.
- He will lead a new global world power and will hold power for a length of time determined by God.
- He will speak blasphemies against God and attempt to subvert God's laws and the natural order.
- He will make war upon the saints of God and will succeed for a time.
- He will be judged by God and cast into the lake of fire along with Satan.

While all four of the beast-nations are world superpowers during their apex, this fourth beast-empire of the Antichrist covers the entire world. It stands in direct conflict with God and will ultimately be destroyed by Him:

"I beheld then because of the voice of the great words which the horn spake: I beheld even till the beast was slain, and his body destroyed, and given to the burning flame."
Daniel 7:11

These are serious things, and I am sure some of them are hard to believe. We will be discussing many things from this point forward which are going to be hard to read (and hard for me to write). I would strongly encourage you to consider these passages of

Scripture for yourself as we proceed. Find a good Bible (I would recommend the time-proven King James Version) and follow along as we continue. Prove these things for yourself. And if you do not know God, please consider this promise that He has given to us in the writings of the prophet Jeremiah:

"And ye shall seek me, and find me, when ye shall search for me with all your heart."
Jeremiah 29:13

Chapter 2: The Fall of Ancient Babylon

Daniel 5

~

"Daniel answered and said, Blessed be the name of God for ever and ever: for wisdom and might are his:

And he changeth the times and the seasons: he removeth kings, and setteth up kings: he giveth wisdom unto the wise, and knowledge to them that know understanding:

He revealeth the deep and secret things: he knoweth what is in the darkness, and the light dwelleth with him."

Daniel 2:20-22

The Writing on the Wall in Daniel 5

Before continuing beyond the Biblical book of Daniel, I feel it will serve us well to take a moment to discuss the fall of ancient Babylon. The Bible has a great deal to say about the fall of Babylon, but when we compare the fall of ancient Babylon to the fall of "Babylon" in Biblical prophecy, things do not seem to add up. We begin to realize that much of the Biblical prophecy is actually referring to *Mystery Babylon*, and not the ancient Neo-Babylonian Empire. A short overview of ancient Babylon's conquest by the Medes and Persians will therefore be useful as a point of reference as we continue on in later chapters to study other Biblical books' prophecies concerning Mystery Babylon and its future destruction. (We will see conclusively in Chapter 3 that ancient Babylon and Jeremiah's Babylon are not the same nation.)

The "fall of Babylon" generally refers to the end of the Neo-Babylonian Empire due to its conquest and assimilation into the Medo-Persian (or Achaemenid) Empire. Nabonidus was king of Babylon at its fall, co-ruling with his son Belshazzar, and was a descendant of the Nebuchadnezzar of the first several chapters of the book of Daniel. Babylon's fall occurs between the events of chapters 5 and 6 of Daniel. The Biblical account, being more focused on the theme of God's omniscience and rulership over history, lacks a great deal of contextual background information and even omits any substantial account of the actual fall itself of the city and empire of Babylon.

We know historically that Darius the Mede and Cyrus the Persian (Cyrus the Great) formed a compact and assaulted the Babylonian Empire, likely laying siege to the capital city of Babylon itself. An ancient siege, while certainly a serious predicament, was a fairly common occurrence and cities were heavily fortified and provisioned so that they might outlast a prolonged siege for years or even decades. Sieges were expensive operations, with the besieging armies requiring provisions and materials for constructing engines of war. Babylon was reknowned in the ancient world for its massive impenetrable walls and gates, and situated as it was on the river Euphrates, it had an unlimited supply of fresh water. In situations like this, diplomacy or rescue by friendly forces would likely break the siege before the city could fall to the invaders, especially since king Nabonidus was elsewhere in the empire at the time while his son and co-ruler Belshazzar managed the empire from the capital city of Babylon. This system of co-regents was exceedingly common in the ancient world and may actually have been the normal *modus operandii* for some civilizations. We see it employed elsewhere, such as in ancient Egypt, where often two rulers administrated simultaneously from capital cities in Upper and Lower Egypt. Such a system of dual rulership allowed a younger future monarch to gain practical skills and experience in the affairs of state.

Daniel chapter 5 does not mention this siege, but it does tell us that Belshazzar held a great feast for a thousand of his nobles:

"Belshazzar the king made a great feast to a thousand of his lords, and drank wine before the thousand.

Belshazzar, whiles he tasted the wine, commanded to bring the golden and silver vessels which his father Nebuchadnezzar had taken out of the temple which was in Jerusalem; that the king, and his princes, his wives, and his concubines, might drink therein.

Then they brought the golden vessels that were taken out of the temple of the house of God which was at Jerusalem; and the king, and his princes, his wives, and his concubines, drank in them.

They drank wine, and praised the gods of gold, and of silver, of brass, of iron, of wood, and of stone."

Daniel 5:1-4

Some sources suggest that Belshazzar's feast was a religious celebration of a Babylonian moon deity. This makes sense on several levels, even if Babylon was currently besieged by the Medes and Persians; there was a need to keep up morale and appearances, and a need to please the gods in order to curry their favor against Babylon's enemies. This is exactly what we see in Daniel 5; Belshazzar, as if to remind his followers of the supremacy of their Babylonian gods over all other gods, commanded that the toasts to their idols should be drunk from the sacred temple vessels of the God of a conquered people: the Jews. The command was an extravagant posturing gesture, and it might have been a great morale booster for the Babylonians if Balshazzar had chosen some other conquered pagan deity to humiliate instead of the true God of Heaven. A near immediate response to Belshazzar's hubris manifested itself:

"In the same hour came forth fingers of a man's hand, and wrote over against the candlestick upon the plaister of the wall of the king's palace: and the king saw

the part of the hand that wrote.

Then the king's countenance was changed, and his thoughts troubled him, so that the joints of his loins were loosed, and his knees smote one against another.

The king cried aloud to bring in the astrologers, the Chaldeans, and the soothsayers. And the king spake, and said to the wise men of Babylon, Whosoever shall read this writing, and shew me the interpretation thereof, shall be clothed with scarlet, and have a chain of gold about his neck, and shall be the third ruler in the kingdom.

Then came in all the king's wise men: but they could not read the writing, nor make known to the king the interpretation thereof.

Then was king Belshazzar greatly troubled, and his countenance was changed in him, and his lords were astonied."

Daniel 5:5-9

The banquet was not going as planned. Belshazzar instantly knew that something had gone horribly wrong, and he nearly lost control of his bowels and could not keep himself from shaking. The nobles of Babylon were likewise stricken with terror. An interpreter was needed to make plain the message on the wall, and in a panic Belshazzar called out for all the best scientific advisors of the day. The usual procession of pandering lapdogs trooped into the banquet hall: the astrologers, the Chaldeans, and the soothsayers. None of their arts or wisdom could give the king an interpretation of the supernatural writing. But an answer was not far off; the queen had heard the commotion and had a recommendation:

"Now the queen, by reason of the words of the king and his lords, came into the banquet house: and the queen spake and said, O king, live for ever: let not thy thoughts trouble thee, nor let thy countenance be changed:

There is a man in thy kingdom, in whom is the spirit of the holy gods; and in the days of thy father light and understanding and wisdom, like the wisdom of the gods, was found in him; whom the king Nebuchadnezzar thy father, the king, I say, thy father, made master of the magicians, astrologers, Chaldeans, and soothsayers;

Forasmuch as an excellent spirit, and knowledge, and understanding, interpreting of dreams, and shewing of hard sentences, and dissolving of doubts, were found in the same Daniel, whom the king named Belteshazzar: now let Daniel be called, and he will shew the interpretation.

Then was Daniel brought in before the king. And the king spake and said unto Daniel, Art thou that Daniel, which art of the children of the captivity of Judah, whom the king my father brought out of Jewry?

I have even heard of thee, that the spirit of the gods is in thee, and that light and understanding and excellent wisdom is found in thee.

And now the wise men, the astrologers, have been brought in before me, that they should read this writing, and make known unto me the interpretation thereof: but they could not shew the interpretation of the thing:

And I have heard of thee, that thou canst make interpretations, and dissolve doubts: now if thou canst read the writing, and make known to me the interpretation thereof, thou shalt be clothed with scarlet, and have a chain of gold about thy neck, and shalt be the third ruler in the kingdom."

Daniel 5:10-16

Due to her familiarity with the events of Nebuchadnezzar's reign as recorded earlier in the book of Daniel, it is likely that this queen of Babylon was not Belshazzar's own wife but a prior queen, perhaps even the wife of Nebuchadnezzar. (The two kings who followed Nebuchadnezzar and who preceded Nabonidas and Belshazzar had exceedingly short reigns.) The usage of the term "thy father" in this passage is similar to the Biblical use of "Father Abraham" by the Jews -- an acknowledgement that Nebuchadnezzar was Belshazzar's ancestor and forebear, not of actual immediate parentage. Notice also that the reward offered to Daniel was the position of *third* ruler in the kingdom of Babylon; Belshazzar himself was only the second ruler, under his father Nabonidus, and could not offer a position higher than that of number three.

But it seems that Daniel already knew the interpretation of the writing on the wall; perhaps he had seen it previously in another night vision. He minces no words and rejects the king's offer of position, and immediately gives Belshazzar the interpretation of the writing:

"Then Daniel answered and said before the king, Let thy gifts be to thyself, and give thy rewards to another;

yet I will read the writing unto the king, and make known to him the interpretation.

O thou king, the most high God gave Nebuchadnezzar thy father a kingdom, and majesty, and glory, and honour:

And for the majesty that he gave him, all people, nations, and languages, trembled and feared before him: whom he would he slew; and whom he would he kept alive; and whom he would he set up; and whom he would he put down.

But when his heart was lifted up, and his mind hardened in pride, he was deposed from his kingly throne, and they took his glory from him:

And he was driven from the sons of men; and his heart was made like the beasts, and his dwelling was with the wild asses: they fed him with grass like oxen, and his body was wet with the dew of heaven; till he knew that the most high God ruled in the kingdom of men, and that he appointeth over it whomsoever he will.

And thou his son, O Belshazzar, hast not humbled thine heart, though thou knewest all this;

But hast lifted up thyself against the Lord of heaven; and they have brought the vessels of his house before thee, and thou, and thy lords, thy wives, and thy concubines, have drunk wine in them; and thou hast praised the gods of silver, and gold, of brass, iron, wood, and stone, which see not, nor hear, nor know: and the God in whose hand thy breath is, and whose are all thy ways, hast thou not glorified:

Then was the part of the hand sent from him; and this writing was written.

And this is the writing that was written, MENE, MENE, TEKEL, UPHARSIN.

This is the interpretation of the thing: MENE; God hath numbered thy kingdom, and finished it.

TEKEL; Thou art weighed in the balances, and art found wanting.

PERES; Thy kingdom is divided, and given to the Medes and Persians."

Daniel 5:17-28

King Belshazzar, second ruler of Babylon, had been weighed in the balances by the God of Heaven and had been found lacking. Daniel's accusation in Daniel 5:22-23 rang in his ears: Belshazzar had known about the God of Heaven from accounts of his ancestor Nebuchadnezzar, but he had chosen to mock God and exalt the powerless Babylonian idols of silver, gold, brass, iron, wood, and stone regardless. God's sentence had been issued; the sun had already set upon the mighty Babylonian Empire. Sickened, but with the need to keep up appearances, Belshazzar gave to Daniel the rewards which he had promised, rewards which were now utterly meaningless in light of what was about to happen next:

"Then commanded Belshazzar, and they clothed Daniel with scarlet, and put a chain of gold about his neck, and made a proclamation concerning him, that he should be the third ruler in the kingdom.

In that night was Belshazzar the king of the Chaldeans slain.

And Darius the Median took the kingdom, being about threescore and two years old."
Daniel 5:29-31

The book of Daniel does not go into much further detail concerning the fall of ancient Babylon, but we will see in a moment from the beginning of Daniel 6 (and most other historical sources agree) that it was a largely bloodless takeover by the Medo-Persians. Two decades ago (in Sunday school) I was taught one of the prevailing theories concerning Babylon's fall, which is that the besieging Persian armies diverted the Euphrates river from its course and entered the city of Babylon through the dry waterway. Other historians have suggested that one of the gates of the city was either forcibly destroyed or opened through treachery or subterfuge. Whatever the case, the surrounding armies gained ingress and made their way through the streets of the city, killing what little resistance they encountered; Babylon's soldiers and populace were largely intoxicated due to the lunar festival. The Persian troops were able to easily access the palace and most of the noble revelers there were also intoxicated and unarmed; while some attempted to defend themselves with whatever came to hand, most were quickly cut down, including King Belshazzar himself. Daniel 6 notes the easy transition of the empire from Babylonian lordship to Medo-Persian control:

"It pleased Darius to set over the kingdom an

hundred and twenty princes, which should be over the whole kingdom;

And over these three presidents; of whom Daniel was first: that the princes might give accounts unto them, and the king should have no damage."

Daniel 6:1-2

Babylon was now a province of the Medo-Persian Empire under the co-rule of Darius the Mede and Cyrus the Persian. Darius, likely the more senior of the two rulers, was desirous that the transition of rule should proceed as smoothly as possible; thus we see him utilizing the existing Babylonian administration to rule over the newly acquired territory in Daniel chapter 6. Other historic sources tell us that Nabonidus was also eventually captured by the Persians and remained a well-treated captive for the rest of his days.

Cyrus the Persian, Darius' co-regent, is a particularly interesting figure, since he is the subject of Biblical prophecy as well. The prophet Isaiah wrote about Cyrus by name more than a century before Cyrus was born:

"Thus saith the LORD, thy redeemer, and he that formed thee from the womb, I am the LORD that maketh all things; that stretcheth forth the heavens alone; that spreadeth abroad the earth by myself;

That frustrateth the tokens of the liars, and maketh diviners mad; that turneth wise men backward, and maketh their knowledge foolish;

That confirmeth the word of his servant, and performeth the counsel of his messengers; that saith to Jerusalem, Thou shalt be inhabited; and to the cities of Judah, Ye shall be built, and I will raise up the decayed places thereof:

That saith to the deep, Be dry, and I will dry up thy rivers:

That saith of Cyrus, He is my shepherd, and shall perform all my pleasure: even saying to Jerusalem, Thou shalt be built; and to the temple, Thy foundation shall be laid.

Thus saith the LORD to his anointed, to Cyrus, whose right hand I have holden, to subdue nations before him*; and I will loose the loins of kings, to open before him the two leaved gates; and the gates shall not be shut;*

I will go before thee, and make the crooked places straight: I will break in pieces the gates of brass, and cut in sunder the bars of iron:

And I will give thee the treasures of darkness, and hidden riches of secret places, ***that thou mayest know that I, the LORD, which call thee by thy name, am the God of Israel.****"*

Isaiah 44:24-45:3

Indeed all that Isaiah prophesied concerning Cyrus would come to pass; Cyrus the Great would free the Jews held in captivity in Babylon and issue an edict to rebuild the temple at Jerusalem. Cyrus ordered that the Jewish temple vessels be returned, and astoundingly Cyrus even funded the temple building endeavor from his own treasury:

"Then Darius the king made a decree, and search was made in the house of the rolls, where the treasures were laid up in Babylon.

And there was found at Achmetha, in the palace that is in the province of the Medes, a roll, and therein was a record thus written:

In the first year of Cyrus the king the same Cyrus the king made a decree concerning the house of God at Jerusalem, Let the house be builded, the place where they offered sacrifices, and let the foundations thereof be strongly laid; the height thereof threescore cubits, and the breadth thereof threescore cubits;

With three rows of great stones, and a row of new timber: and let the expenses be given out of the king's house:

And also let the golden and silver vessels of the house of God, which Nebuchadnezzar took forth out of the temple which is at Jerusalem, and brought unto Babylon, be restored, and brought again unto the temple which is at Jerusalem, every one to his place, and place them in the house of God."

Ezra 6:1-5

And what became of the prophet Daniel? The Bible tells us that "this Daniel prospered in the reign of Darius, and in the reign of Cyrus the Persian." (Daniel 6:28)

The great city of Babylon survived the end of

the Neo-Babylonian Empire and would be an important city during the time of numerous subsequent powers in the region. Portions were rebuilt on sections of the older city beneath them, as was common practice in the ancient world. A community and a church existed at Babylon shortly after the time of Christ, according to the New Testament epistle of 1 Peter: "The church that is at Babylon, elected together with you, saluteth you; and so does Marcus my son." (1 Peter 5:13)

As rivers shifted and the city changed hands, Babylon slowly dried up and was lost to time. Local peoples scavenged the ruins for bricks to use as building materials. In modern times, archaeologists studied and excavated portions of the complex and extensive ruins of the city, and eventually Saddam Hussein would rebuild large portions of it. In the next chapter as we look at the prophet Jeremiah and his writings concerning the fall of Babylon, I hope you will pay close attention, as the description of Babylon's utter, rapid destruction laid out in the book of Jeremiah simply does not match what we have just discussed concerning the downfall of ancient Babylon.

"These were more noble than those in Thessalonica, in that they received the word with all readiness of mind, and searched the scriptures daily, whether those things were so."

Acts 17:11

Chapter 3:
Jeremiah's Babylon Is Not Ancient Babylon

Jeremiah 50 and 51

~

"This know also, that in the last days perilous times shall come.

For men shall be lovers of their own selves, covetous, boasters, proud, blasphemers, disobedient to parents, unthankful, unholy,

Without natural affection, trucebreakers, false accusers, incontinent, fierce, despisers of those that are good,

Traitors, heady, highminded, lovers of pleasures more than lovers of God."

2 Timothy 3:1-4

God's Word Against Babylon Through Jeremiah

Having briefly overviewed the fall of the ancient Babylonian Empire, we will now turn to another Biblical prophet: Jeremiah. Two full chapters of the book of Jeremiah contain a lengthy and detailed description of the sudden and violent destruction of Babylon as forewarned by God and dictated through His prophet Jeremiah.

As I have mentioned in prior chapters, the details contained in Jeremiah chapters 50 and 51 are strikingly different from the picture of ancient Babylon's fall that we see in the book of Daniel and through other historical sources. It becomes readily apparent that Jeremiah is describing the destruction of some *other* civilization for which ancient Babylon is a symbol or type. This is a prevalent Biblical and prophetic literary device and is used elsewhere in the Scriptures; the most notable example is the use of Egypt to represent the nature of sin. As the Hebrews were enslaved by the Egyptians and even converted to Egyptian religion, so sin enslaves and deceives those who become trapped within its grasp. Ultimately only an act of God can save people shackled by sin; likewise an act of God was required to free the subjugated Hebrews from their Egyptian overlords.

In the case of the Jeremiah prophecies, however, we must not make the mistake of supposing that the type or symbol which Babylon represents in Jeremiah 50 and 51 is purely spiritual or symbolic. While some elements of these chapters might be figurative, there are far too many literal, explicit details and warnings for us to approach this section of Scripture as if it is entirely figurative. No, these chapters clearly represent the destruction of a very real kingdom or nation.

In this book chapter we will survey the entirety of Jeremiah 50 and 51, but our focus will remain on those parts of these chapters which *do not* and *cannot* represent ancient Babylon. Having established a difference between ancient Babylon and Jeremiah's "Babylon," we will return to these chapters of Jeremiah later on and in more detail as we seek to positively identify Mystery Babylon.

Jeremiah chapter 50 begins thusly:

"The word that the LORD spake against Babylon and against the land of the Chaldeans by Jeremiah the prophet.

Declare ye among the nations, and publish, and set up a standard; publish, and conceal not: say, Babylon is taken, Bel is confounded, Merodach is broken in pieces; her idols are confounded, her images are broken in pieces."

Jeremiah 50:1-2

The Neo-Babylonian Empire (of Daniel's day) was ruled by a Chaldean nobility, from which the kings derived. The use of the term "the land of the Chaldeans" is therefore not out of place in an association with ancient Babylon. The term is emphasized over and over again throughout Jeremiah 50 and 51, and it is worth mentioning that there is another connotation to this phrase, especially in light of God's message in Jeremiah 50 verse 2. Remember the sorcerers, soothsayers, astrologers, and their ilk which we met when we discussed Daniel's interpretations in a prior chapter of this book? The term "Chaldean" was included in those lists of all the advisors whose wisdom the Babylonian kings sought because the Chaldean nobility were intelligent and well educated in the knowledge of their time. "Chaldeans" can be synonymous with "the wisest in the land" (as one Bible dictionary puts it), or one who is skilled in human wisdom.

We see a statement of God's intent in the first verses of Jeremiah 50. The utter destruction of Jeremiah's Babylon (whose description follows) is intended by God to serve as a warning for all the nations of the earth who trust in their own wisdom. Jeremiah 50 verse 2 specifically emphasizes the destruction and confounding of Babylon's man-made false gods. In ancient times the success and power of a nation was often attributed to its patron deities; here God is stating that Babylon's destruction shows that her faith was poorly placed in her worthless gods, who could not save her.

"For out of the north there cometh up a nation against her, which shall make her land desolate, and none shall dwell therein: they shall remove, they shall depart, both man and beast.

In those days, and in that time, saith the LORD, the children of Israel shall come, they and the children of Judah together, going and weeping: they shall go, and seek the LORD their God.

They shall ask the way to Zion with their faces thitherward, saying, Come, and let us join ourselves to the LORD in a perpetual covenant that shall not be forgotten."

Jeremiah 50:3-5

Jeremiah 50:3-5 are interesting because they simply cannot represent the fall of ancient Babylon. While the fall of ancient Babylon did indirectly result in the captive Jews being freed to return to their homeland by Cyrus' edict, it seems unlikely that they would weep for their captor Babylon. It could perhaps be argued that these released Jews are weeping tears of joy at their emancipation; but we will see in a moment a verse (verse 8) which will give pause to this thought. And it must be mentioned that ancient Babylon was never "made desolate" by her conquerors, nor did man or beast remove from her and leave her without inhabitants. Even long after the ancient city of Babylon dried up and disappeared, nomadic tribes and small communities still called the immediate area home.

"My people hath been lost sheep: their shepherds have caused them to go astray, they have turned them away on the mountains: they have gone from mountain to hill, they have forgotten their restingplace.

All that found them have devoured them: and their adversaries said, We offend not, because they have sinned against the LORD, the habitation of justice, even the LORD, the hope of their fathers."

Jeremiah 50:6-7

Sadly, we can see from history that the predictions of Jeremiah 50 verses 6 and 7 have been fulfilled over and over again. While the Soviet pogroms and the Nazi Holocaust were perhaps the most blatant abuses of the Jews, God's people have been historically abused and mistrusted wherever they have wandered. Antisemitism is alive and well even today in the modern world. Perhaps even more tragic than this is that the Jews themselves, by-and-large, have forgotten the faith of their fathers.

"Remove out of the midst of Babylon, and go forth out of the land of the Chaldeans, and be as the he goats before the flocks."
Jeremiah 50:8

Jeremiah 50 verse 8 is the first in a series of warnings for God's people to flee Babylon before the coming destruction. It is a significant commandment because it suggests an autonomy on the part of God's people in Babylon, an autonomy that the Hebrew captives simply did not possess during their captivity in ancient Babylon. As slaves, the Jews could not simply decide to return to their homeland. This command seems out of place if the Babylon of Jeremiah 50 and 51 is meant to be ancient Babylon. We will see later that this is not the only such command to flee Babylon in order to survive the wrath to come. As mentioned above, it would seem that the Jews living in Jeremiah's Babylon weep at her destruction and are hesitant to leave her though they have the freedom to do so.

"For, lo, I will raise and cause to come up against Babylon an assembly of great nations from the north country: and they shall set themselves in array against her; from thence she shall be taken: their arrows shall be as of a mighty expert man; none shall return in vain.

And Chaldea shall be a spoil: all that spoil her shall be satisfied, saith the LORD.

Because ye were glad, because ye rejoiced, O ye destroyers of mine heritage, because ye are grown fat as the heifer at grass, and bellow as bulls;

Your mother shall be sore confounded; she that bare you shall be ashamed: behold, the hindermost of the nations shall be a wilderness, a dry land, and a desert.

Because of the wrath of the LORD it shall not be inhabited, but it shall be wholly desolate: every one that goeth by Babylon shall be astonished, and hiss at all her plagues.

Put yourselves in array against Babylon round about: all ye that bend the bow, shoot at her, spare no arrows: for she hath sinned against the LORD.

Shout against her round about: she hath given her hand: her foundations are fallen, her walls are thrown down: for it is the vengeance of the LORD: take vengeance upon her; as she hath done, do unto her.

Cut off the sower from Babylon, and him that handleth the sickle in the time of harvest: for fear of the oppressing sword they shall turn every one to his people, and they shall flee every one to his own land."

Jeremiah 50:9-16

Again, much of Jeremiah 50:9-16 simply does not fit with the fall of ancient Babylon. Perhaps the Medes and Persians could be considered "an assembly of great nations," but their origins lay to the east of Babylon, not the north. The physical assault on Babylon (especially the use of arrows, which is reiterated several times in Jeremiah 50 and 51), the spoiling of Chaldea, the land being reduced to a barren wilderness -- these things simply cannot be said of ancient Babylon's fall. Do all who pass by Babylon sneer at the utter destruction that has befallen her? Is the region entirely unpopulated? No, rather the slow decline and fading away of Babylon over centuries is quite similar to the slow decline of many other lost ancient cities, not at all unique or astonishing, and ancient Babylon's walls and foundations were not utterly cast down. Jeremiah 50:16 alludes to a large population of many ethnic groups living within Jeremiah's Babylon (as migrant agricultural workers); as violence overshadows the land, they flee to their own countries.

"Israel is a scattered sheep; the lions have driven him away: first the king of Assyria hath devoured him; and last this Nebuchadrezzar king of Babylon hath broken his bones.

Therefore thus saith the LORD of hosts, the God of Israel; Behold, I will punish the king of Babylon and his land, as I have punished the king of Assyria.

And I will bring Israel again to his habitation, and he shall feed on Carmel and Bashan, and his soul shall be satisfied upon mount Ephraim and Gilead.

In those days, and in that time, saith the LORD, the iniquity of Israel shall be sought for, and there shall be none; and the sins of Judah, and they shall not be found: for I will pardon them whom I reserve."

Jeremiah 50:17-20

Here we see that Assyria and Babylon are guilty in God's estimation for their treatment of His people Israel. The destruction of Jeremiah's Babylon will be used by God to draw more of the scattered Jews back to Israel and into communion with their God.

"Go up against the land of Merathaim, even against it, and against the inhabitants of Pekod: waste and utterly destroy after them, saith the LORD, and do according to all that I have commanded thee.

A sound of battle is in the land, and of great destruction."

Jeremiah 50:21-22

There is some debate amongst Bible scholars as to the exact meaning of the term "Merathaim." While the word has the connotation of both "double rebellion" and "double bitterness," some scholars argue that it is a specific place-name. I feel it may well be a figurative term based on the numerous Biblical references (many of which will be discussed later in this book) to Mystery Babylon being a nation which has raised itself up against God Himself, and therefore God will render to her double punishment for the things she has done (Revelation 18:6). The meaning of the term "Pekod" is likewise contested; it has the connotation of "visitation" or "judgment." The appearance of these two terms so close to each other, and the inability of scholars to conclusively identify them as specific places, seems to suggest that these terms are poetic and prophetic, not actual locations.

"How is the hammer of the whole earth cut asunder and broken! how is Babylon become a desolation among the nations!

I have laid a snare for thee, and thou art also taken, O Babylon, and thou wast not aware: thou art found, and also caught, because thou hast striven against the LORD.

The LORD hath opened his armoury, and hath brought forth the weapons of his indignation: for this is the work of the Lord GOD of hosts in the land of the Chaldeans."

Jeremiah 50:23-25

Here we have mention of Mystery Babylon's rebellion against God. Mystery Babylon has been one of God's tools against the nations of the whole earth, but her victory caused her to raise herself up in pride against God's laws. She will not be a weapon in God's hand any longer; He does not need her to enact His will in the earth. The God of Heaven will open His own arsenal in order to judge Babylon.

"Come against her from the utmost border, open

her storehouses: cast her up as heaps, and destroy her utterly: let nothing of her be left.

Slay all her bullocks; let them go down to the slaughter: woe unto them! for their day is come, the time of their visitation.

The voice of them that flee and escape out of the land of Babylon, to declare in Zion the vengeance of the LORD our God, the vengeance of his temple.

Call together the archers against Babylon: all ye that bend the bow, camp against it round about; let none thereof escape: recompense her according to her work; according to all that she hath done, do unto her: for she hath been proud against the LORD, against the Holy One of Israel.

Therefore shall her young men fall in the streets, and all her men of war shall be cut off in that day, saith the LORD."

Jeremiah 50:26-30

Here in Jeremiah 50:26-30 we have an overview of the destruction which will overtake Mystery Babylon; she will be utterly plundered and destroyed on all sides, her cattle slain, her young people will die in the streets, and her military will be utterly discomfited. Notice that this does not describe the capture of ancient Babylon by Darius and Cyrus in the slightest. These verses, and the next, emphasize that Jeremiah's Babylon will be judged for her own works and for her pride:

"Behold, I am against thee, O thou most proud,

saith the Lord GOD of hosts: for thy day is come, the time that I will visit thee.

And the most proud shall stumble and fall, and none shall raise him up: and I will kindle a fire in his cities, and it shall devour all round about him.

Thus saith the LORD of hosts; The children of Israel and the children of Judah were oppressed together: and all that took them captives held them fast; they refused to let them go.

Their Redeemer is strong; the LORD of hosts is his name: he shall throughly plead their cause, that he may give rest to the land, and disquiet the inhabitants of Babylon."

Jeremiah 50:31-34

Above we also see a reference to the destruction of Jeremiah's Babylon by fire, one of many such references to Mystery Babylon's burning, and another detail which is not applicable to ancient Babylon. Jeremiah continues with an overview of all the various people who will taste God's wrath during the judgment of Babylon:

"A sword is upon the Chaldeans, saith the LORD, and upon the inhabitants of Babylon, and upon her princes, and upon her wise men.

A sword is upon the liars; and they shall dote: a sword is upon her mighty men; and they shall be dismayed.

A sword is upon their horses, and upon their chariots, and upon all the mingled people that are in the midst of her; and they shall become as women: a sword is

upon her treasures; and they shall be robbed."
Jeremiah 50:35-37

Riches, leaders, advisors, scheming politicians, and armies -- none of these shall turn away God's destruction from Jeremiah's Babylon. The judgment will be so absolute that Mystery Babylon will be reduced to a barren wasteland without water or human inhabitants:

"A drought is upon her waters; and they shall be dried up: for it is the land of graven images, and they are mad upon their idols.

Therefore the wild beasts of the desert with the wild beasts of the islands shall dwell there, and the owls shall dwell therein: and it shall be no more inhabited for ever; neither shall it be dwelt in from generation to generation.

As God overthrew Sodom and Gomorrah and the neighbour cities thereof, saith the LORD; so shall no man abide there, neither shall any son of man dwell therein."
Jeremiah 50:38-40

This destruction will be enacted by a great coalition of northern nations:

"Behold, a people shall come from the north, and a great nation, and many kings shall be raised up from the coasts of the earth.

They shall hold the bow and the lance: they are cruel, and will not shew mercy: their voice shall roar like the sea, and they shall ride upon horses, every one put in array, like a man to the battle, against thee, O daughter of Babylon.

The king of Babylon hath heard the report of them, and his hands waxed feeble: anguish took hold of him, and pangs as of a woman in travail.

Behold, he shall come up like a lion from the swelling of Jordan unto the habitation of the strong: but I will make them suddenly run away from her: and who is a chosen man, that I may appoint over her? for who is like me? and who will appoint me the time ? and who is that shepherd that will stand before me?

Therefore hear ye the counsel of the LORD, that he hath taken against Babylon; and his purposes, that he hath purposed against the land of the Chaldeans: Surely the least of the flock shall draw them out: surely he shall make their habitation desolate with them.

At the noise of the taking of Babylon the earth is moved, and the cry is heard among the nations."

Jeremiah 50:41-46

The first verses of Jeremiah 51 once again detail the destruction of Jeremiah's Babylon by fire and arrows. We see that this is an unnatural flame, like the fire and brimstone (sulphur) sent to destroy Sodom and Gomorrah. It is interesting to note here that the *arrows* sent against Mystery Babylon are specifically targeting her own *archers* and *defenses*:

"Thus saith the LORD; Behold, I will raise up against Babylon, and against them that dwell in the midst

of them that rise up against me, a destroying wind;

And will send unto Babylon fanners, that shall fan her, and shall empty her land: for in the day of trouble they shall be against her round about.

Against him that bendeth let the archer bend his bow, and against him that lifteth himself up in his brigandine: and spare ye not her young men; destroy ye utterly all her host.

Thus the slain shall fall in the land of the Chaldeans, and they that are thrust through in her streets."

Jeremiah 51:1-4

In Jeremiah 51:6, we have another warning to God's people living within Mystery Babylon to flee out of her in order to survive the coming judgment:

"For Israel hath not been forsaken, nor Judah of his God, of the LORD of hosts; though their land was filled with sin against the Holy One of Israel.

Flee out of the midst of Babylon, and deliver every man his soul: be not cut off in her iniquity; for this is the time of the LORD'S vengeance; he will render unto her a recompence.

Babylon hath been a golden cup in the LORD'S hand, that made all the earth drunken: the nations have drunken of her wine; therefore the nations are mad.

Babylon is suddenly fallen and destroyed: howl for her; take balm for her pain, if so be she may be healed.

We would have healed Babylon, but she is not

healed: forsake her, and let us go every one into his own country: for her judgment reacheth unto heaven, and is lifted up even to the skies.

The LORD hath brought forth our righteousness: come, and let us declare in Zion the work of the LORD our God."

Jeremiah 51:5-10

Jeremiah 51:7-10 are clear that it will be obvious that Babylon's destruction was ordained and ochestrated by God. God's people who survive that nation's fall will preach His righteousness to the nations. But Jeremiah is far from finished:

"Make bright the arrows; gather the shields: the LORD hath raised up the spirit of the kings of the Medes: for his device is against Babylon, to destroy it; because it is the vengeance of the LORD, the vengeance of his temple.

Set up the standard upon the walls of Babylon, make the watch strong, set up the watchmen, prepare the ambushes: for the LORD hath both devised and done that which he spake against the inhabitants of Babylon.

O thou that dwellest upon many waters, abundant in treasures, thine end is come, and the measure of thy covetousness.

The LORD of hosts hath sworn by himself, saying, Surely I will fill thee with men, as with caterpillers; and they shall lift up a shout against thee.

He hath made the earth by his power, he hath established the world by his wisdom, and hath stretched out the heaven by his understanding.

When he uttereth his voice, there is a multitude of waters in the heavens; and he causeth the vapours to ascend from the ends of the earth: he maketh lightnings with rain, and bringeth forth the wind out of his treasures.

Every man is brutish by his knowledge; every founder is confounded by the graven image: for his molten image is falsehood, and there is no breath in them.

They are vanity, the work of errors: in the time of their visitation they shall perish.

The portion of Jacob is not like them; for he is the former of all things: and Israel is the rod of his inheritance: the LORD of hosts is his name."

Jeremiah 51:11-19

In the above verses we see that while Babylon is mighty and fortifies herself against any aggression, the Lord of Hosts is greater and wiser, and He has sworn in His own Name that He will destroy Mystery Babylon. Bayblon's devices and preparations will be no match against God's plans and purpose against her. God will win because Babylon has merely been a tool in His hand:

"Thou art my battle axe and weapons of war: for with thee will I break in pieces the nations, and with thee will I destroy kingdoms;

And with thee will I break in pieces the horse and his rider; and with thee will I break in pieces the chariot and his rider;

With thee also will I break in pieces man and woman; and with thee will I break in pieces old and young;

and with thee will I break in pieces the young man and the maid;

I will also break in pieces with thee the shepherd and his flock; and with thee will I break in pieces the husbandman and his yoke of oxen; and with thee will I break in pieces captains and rulers.

And I will render unto Babylon and to all the inhabitants of Chaldea all their evil that they have done in Zion in your sight, saith the LORD.

Behold, I am against thee, O destroying mountain, saith the LORD, which destroyest all the earth: and I will stretch out mine hand upon thee, and roll thee down from the rocks, and will make thee a burnt mountain.

And they shall not take of thee a stone for a corner, nor a stone for foundations; but thou shalt be desolate for ever, saith the LORD."

Jeremiah 51:20-26

Notice that Jeremiah 51:26 makes it explicitly clear that the prophet is not describing ancient Babylon. Bricks from ancient Babylon were scavenged by local peoples for centuries to use in their own building projects. This was a very common practice and remains so to this day. Jeremiah's Babylon will be so utterly reduced to desolation that there will be no one left to scavenge building materials from her ruins.

Jeremiah continues with a list describing the various nations which will rise up and perpetrate all this destruction upon Babylon:

Set ye up a standard in the land, blow the trumpet

among the nations, prepare the nations against her, call together against her the kingdoms of Ararat, Minni, and Ashchenaz; appoint a captain against her; cause the horses to come up as the rough caterpillers.

Prepare against her the nations with the kings of the Medes, the captains thereof, and all the rulers thereof, and all the land of his dominion."

Jeremiah 51:27

Notice that the nations of this coalition are different than the Medo-Persian alliance of Darius and Cyrus which assumed control of ancient Babylon. We will discuss these nations in more detail in a later chapter, but this list likely represents the nations of Turkey ("Ararat"), Russia ("Ashchenaz"), and Iran (which now dominates the region which was once the kingdom of the Medes), as well as several other satellite nations of these three.

And the land shall tremble and sorrow: for every purpose of the LORD shall be performed against Babylon, to make the land of Babylon a desolation without an inhabitant.

The mighty men of Babylon have forborn to fight, they have remained in their holds: their might hath failed; they became as women: they have burned her dwellingplaces; her bars are broken.

One post shall run to meet another, and one messenger to meet another, to shew the king of Babylon that his city is taken at one end,

And that the passages are stopped, and the reeds

they have burned with fire, and the men of war are affrighted.

For thus saith the LORD of hosts, the God of Israel; The daughter of Babylon is like a threshingfloor, it is time to thresh her: yet a little while, and the time of her harvest shall come.

Nebuchadrezzar the king of Babylon hath devoured me, he hath crushed me, he hath made me an empty vessel, he hath swallowed me up like a dragon, he hath filled his belly with my delicates, he hath cast me out.

The violence done to me and to my flesh be upon Babylon, shall the inhabitant of Zion say; and my blood upon the inhabitants of Chaldea, shall Jerusalem say.

Therefore thus saith the LORD; Behold, I will plead thy cause, and take vengeance for thee; and I will dry up her sea, and make her springs dry.

And Babylon shall become heaps, a dwellingplace for dragons, an astonishment, and an hissing, without an inhabitant."

Jeremiah 51:29-37

As Jeremiah's Babylon falls, a terror will grip the inhabitants of the land and they will be unable to counterattack their enemies. Every intention of the Lord will come to pass, and Mystery Babylon will be reduced to a barren wasteland inhabited only by scavenging wild animals.

"They shall roar together like lions: they shall yell as lions' whelps.

In their heat I will make their feasts, and I will

make them drunken, that they may rejoice, and sleep a perpetual sleep, and not wake, saith the LORD.

I will bring them down like lambs to the slaughter, like rams with he goats.

How is Sheshach taken! and how is the praise of the whole earth surprised! how is Babylon become an astonishment among the nations!

The sea is come up upon Babylon: she is covered with the multitude of the waves thereof.

Her cities are a desolation, a dry land, and a wilderness, a land wherein no man dwelleth, neither doth any son of man pass thereby.

And I will punish Bel in Babylon, and I will bring forth out of his mouth that which he hath swallowed up: and the nations shall not flow together any more unto him: yea, the wall of Babylon shall fall."

Jeremiah 51:38-44

The citizens of mighty Babylon, once the praise of the whole earth, will watch in dismay as their nation crumbles around them. Many will perhaps embrace alcohol or hedonism to dull their suffering and terror as the end approaches. Immigrants to the nation will try to flee; Jeremiah's Babylon will no longer be an attractive place into which to emigrate.

Jeremiah gives yet another warning to the people of God to know the times and flee out of Mystery Babylon as the time of her judgment approaches:

"My people, go ye out of the midst of her, and deliver ye every man his soul from the fierce anger of the LORD.

And lest your heart faint, and ye fear for the rumour that shall be heard in the land; a rumour shall both come one year, and after that in another year shall come a rumour, and violence in the land, ruler against ruler.

Therefore, behold, the days come, that I will do judgment upon the graven images of Babylon: and her whole land shall be confounded, and all her slain shall fall in the midst of her.

Then the heaven and the earth, and all that is therein, shall sing for Babylon: for the spoilers shall come unto her from the north, saith the LORD."

Jeremiah 51:45-48

Jeremiah admonishes God's people who survive the destruction of Babylon to remember the lessons of that nation's fall and to look towards Jerusalem:

"As Babylon hath caused the slain of Israel to fall, so at Babylon shall fall the slain of all the earth.

Ye that have escaped the sword, go away, stand not still: remember the LORD afar off, and let Jerusalem come into your mind.

We are confounded, because we have heard reproach: shame hath covered our faces: for strangers are come into the sanctuaries of the LORD'S house."

Jeremiah 51:49-51

It will be hard for the citizens of Mystery Babylon to accept that their country is about to experience divine judgment. Her technology and prestige, her wealth, and her military might make her seem unshakeable. But God has sworn that the days of her judgment by fire are coming:

"Wherefore, behold, the days come, saith the LORD, that I will do judgment upon her graven images: and through all her land the wounded shall groan.

Though Babylon should mount up to heaven, and though she should fortify the height of her strength, yet from me shall spoilers come unto her, saith the LORD.

A sound of a cry cometh from Babylon, and great destruction from the land of the Chaldeans:

Because the LORD hath spoiled Babylon, and destroyed out of her the great voice; when her waves do roar like great waters, a noise of their voice is uttered:

Because the spoiler is come upon her, even upon Babylon, and her mighty men are taken, every one of their bows is broken: for the LORD God of recompences shall surely requite.

And I will make drunk her princes, and her wise men, her captains, and her rulers, and her mighty men: and they shall sleep a perpetual sleep, and not wake, saith the King, whose name is the LORD of hosts.

Thus saith the LORD of hosts; The broad walls of Babylon shall be utterly broken, and her high gates shall be burned with fire; and the people shall labour in vain, and

the folk in the fire, and they shall be weary."
Jeremiah 51:52-58

Finally at the end of all his writings, the prophet Jeremiah ordered that a copy of his prophecy be bound to a stone and cast into the river Euphrates, a symbol of the future sinking of Babylon, never to rise again:

"The word which Jeremiah the prophet commanded Seraiah the son of Neriah, the son of Maaseiah, when he went with Zedekiah the king of Judah into Babylon in the fourth year of his reign. And this Seraiah was a quiet prince.

So Jeremiah wrote in a book all the evil that should come upon Babylon, even all these words that are written against Babylon.

And Jeremiah said to Seraiah, When thou comest to Babylon, and shalt see, and shalt read all these words;

Then shalt thou say, O LORD, thou hast spoken against this place, to cut it off, that none shall remain in it, neither man nor beast, but that it shall be desolate for ever.

And it shall be, when thou hast made an end of reading this book, that thou shalt bind a stone to it, and cast it into the midst of Euphrates:

And thou shalt say, ***Thus shall Babylon sink, and shall not rise from the evil that I will bring upon her: and they shall be weary****. Thus far are the words of Jeremiah."* *Jeremiah 51:59-64*

Chapter 4:
Mystery Babylon in the Book of Revelation

Revelation 16:19-19:3

~

"God, who at sundry times and in divers manners spake in time past unto the fathers by the prophets,

Hath in these last days spoken unto us by his Son, whom he hath appointed heir of all things, by whom also he made the worlds."

Hebrews 1:1-2

The Apostle John's Vision of Mystery Babylon

The Biblical book of Revelation was written by the last surviving member of Jesus' original twelve disciples, John, from his exile on the Isle of Patmos. In this book, John recorded the visions that he was given of the end times and the culmination of human history. The book of Revelation was also the final piece of God's revealed Word to humanity, and it was sealed with a curse:

"For I testify unto every man that heareth the words of the prophecy of this book, If any man shall add unto these things, God shall add unto him the plagues that are written in this book:

And if any man shall take away from the words of the book of this prophecy, God shall take away his part out of the book of life, and out of the holy city, and from the things which are written in this book."

Revelation 22:18-19

This is a very serious injunction against changing God's Word; woe to the one who handles God's Word carelessly or maliciously, to either add man's teachings to it, or to take away truth from it! To add to Scripture is to accuse God of forgetting something; and to take away from Scripture is to call God a liar.

Revelation 16:19 through 19:3 describe the destruction of Mystery Babylon. It is here in this passage of Scripture, and only here, that the Bible *explicitly* uses the term "Mystery Babylon":

"And upon her forehead was a name written, MYSTERY, BABYLON THE GREAT, THE MOTHER OF HARLOTS AND ABOMINATIONS OF THE EARTH."

Revelation 17:5

Consider that Mystery Babylon did not yet exist when John had his visions (perhaps around the year AD 70); Revelation makes it plain that Mystery Babylon is a nation and a city existing just prior to the end times. As we consider the text of Revelation 16:19-19:3, you will notice some obvious parallels to things which we have already discussed in Daniel and Jeremiah. We will see later that there are many similarities to the Babylon depicted in Isaiah 47 as well. While the Mystery Babylon of Revelation was presented in a vision and is portrayed in a *spiritual* sense, there are also numerous *physical* details concerning her identity and final destruction.

It should be noted that there are several views concerning the identity and purpose of Mystery Babylon; I will mention these in advance so that you may consider for yourself the relevance of these ideas as we consider these chapters of Revelation. Some people will say that Mystery Babylon is entirely figurative and that it represents the overthrow of wickedness and the world system at the end of days. If this is true, it would seem that John went to a great deal of trouble (for no apparent purpose) to describe the particulars of Mystery Babylon's characteristics and fall in a very roundabout manner. I simply do not think that an honest and straightforward assessment of Revelation can lead to this conclusion. Another camp will assert that Mystery Babylon is the Antichrist's kingdom, the final kingdom upon earth, which will be destroyed by God at the end of time. This position is also untenable, for reasons which we shall discuss in more detail as we consider this passage in Revelation.

The Revelation account of Mystery Babylon

begins thusly:

"And the great city was divided into three parts, and the cities of the nations fell: and great Babylon came in remembrance before God, to give unto her the cup of the wine of the fierceness of his wrath.

And every island fled away, and the mountains were not found.

And there fell upon men a great hail out of heaven, every stone about the weight of a talent: and men blasphemed God because of the plague of the hail; for the plague thereof was exceeding great."

Revelation 16:19-21

The exact chronological order of events in Revelation is difficult to discern, and I will freely assert now that there are details contained in Revelation that simply cannot be fully understood until their fulfillment is actually seen. It would be foolish for me to attempt to dogmatically delineate what all of these details mean or anticipate. Suffice it to say that we see in Revelation 16:19 that at some point in the course of history God will see fit to "remember" Babylon. God is not forgetful as we humans understand forgetfulness; this verse simply means that God will one day decide that the time of merciful forbearance for Mystery Babylon is over, and that it is time for that kingdom's judgment.

We see terrible flooding and hail described in verses 20 and 21, but it is uncertain whether these events are linked to Mystery Babylon's impending destruction, or whether they are associated with the other horrors of the first part of Revelation 16. It would seem (to me) that the mention of Babylon is a mere side note within chapter 16, a bit of foreshadowing, since Babylon's destruction is not actually described until later in Revelation 17 and 18.

In Revelation 17, John is actually given a direct vision of the "Whore of Babylon":

"And there came one of the seven angels which had the seven vials, and talked with me, saying unto me, Come hither; I will shew unto thee the judgment of the great whore that sitteth upon many waters:

With whom the kings of the earth have committed fornication, and the inhabitants of the earth have been made drunk with the wine of her fornication.

So he carried me away in the spirit into the wilderness: and I saw a woman sit upon a scarlet coloured beast, full of names of blasphemy, having seven heads and ten horns.

And the woman was arrayed in purple and scarlet colour, and decked with gold and precious stones and pearls, having a golden cup in her hand full of abominations and filthiness of her fornication:

And upon her forehead was a name written, MYSTERY, BABYLON THE GREAT, THE MOTHER OF HARLOTS AND ABOMINATIONS OF THE EARTH.

And I saw the woman drunken with the blood of the saints, and with the blood of the martyrs of Jesus: and when I saw her, I wondered with great admiration."

Revelation 17:1-6

John sees a vision of Mystery Babylon portrayed as a richly-clad, sensual woman seated upon a wicked beast with ten horns. Several things are immediately apparent from this portion of Scripture; most obviously, one of the chief characteristics of Babylon is sexual immorality: abominations, filthiness, fornication. This nation has not only plunged herself into wanton sexual hedonism, but has spread those appetites to the inhabitants of the whole earth. The Whore of Babylon is intoxicated with the blood of the innocent: God's saints and the martyrs of Jesus Christ.

We have also seen this terrible, ten-horned beast before, in Daniel 7; this beast's association with Mystery Babylon is not mere coincidence. John is stunned by this vision:

"And the angel said unto me, Wherefore didst thou marvel? I will tell thee the mystery of the woman, and of the beast that carrieth her, which hath the seven heads and ten horns.

The beast that thou sawest was, and is not; and shall ascend out of the bottomless pit, and go into perdition: and they that dwell on the earth shall wonder, whose names were not written in the book of life from the foundation of the world, when they behold the beast that was, and is not, and yet is.

And here is the mind which hath wisdom. The seven heads are seven mountains, on which the woman sitteth.

And there are seven kings: five are fallen, and one is, and the other is not yet come; and when he cometh, he must continue a short space.

And the beast that was, and is not, even he is the eighth, and is of the seven, and goeth into perdition.

And the ten horns which thou sawest are ten kings, which have received no kingdom as yet; but receive power as kings one hour with the beast.

These have one mind, and shall give their power and strength unto the beast."

Revelation 17:7-13

Fortunately an angel enlightens John (and us!) as to the meaning of the woman seated upon the beast. The woman's identity is not given immediately; the angel begins with an explanation of the terrible horned beast. We see in verse 8 that the beast's spiritual origins lie within the "bottomless pit" -- this beast and its power are associated with Antichrist and our terrible Adversary, Satan. Sadly, those who will not be God's children will be swayed and mesmerized by this beast.

I think it is quite clear that this is the same beast portrayed in Daniel 7; in Revelation 17:10-13, the angel gives John an account of the rise of the Antichrist's kingdom that parallels the Daniel 7 account of the little horn supplanting three others and taking its place amongst the other horns. The Antichrist's kingdom, the terrible beast-kingdom of Daniel 7 which will overrun the whole earth and make war against God's saints, will be a coalition of nations ruled by the horns (kings). This wicked civilization will be permitted to persist for a time before God overcomes both it and the Antichrist who leads that nation:

"These shall make war with the Lamb, and the Lamb shall overcome them: for he is Lord of lords, and King of kings: and they that are with him are called, and chosen, and faithful."
Revelation 17:14

The angel continues his explanation to John, and makes it *perfectly clear* that Mystery Babylon is *not* the same nation as the terrible beast-kingdom of the Antichrist:

"And he saith unto me, The waters which thou sawest, where the whore sitteth, are peoples, and multitudes, and nations, and tongues.

And the ten horns which thou sawest upon the beast, these shall hate the whore, and shall make her desolate and naked, and shall eat her flesh, and burn her with fire.

For God hath put in their hearts to fulfil his will, and to agree, and give their kingdom unto the beast, until the words of God shall be fulfilled.

And the woman which thou sawest is that great city, which reigneth over the kings of the earth."
Revelation 17:15-18

Again we have a reference to the destruction of Mystery Babylon by fire, and clear verification that the

Whore of Babylon and the horned beast are not the same entity. What are we to make of this? It is apparent that both Mystery Babylon and the horned beast are wicked and guilty enemies of God, and that He will judge them both. These verses make it plain that Mystery Babylon is not the last human nation, as it will be destroyed and replaced by the terrible horned beast, the kingdom of the Antichrist which, according to Daniel 7, will overtake the whole earth.

When we put together all the references to Mystery Babylon from Daniel, Jeremiah, and Revelation, we see that Mystery Babylon is a great power that initially dominates those nations which will one day form the axis of the Antichrist's kingdom. Jeremiah 50 and 51 describe a coalition of great nations from the north that will rise up and destroy Mystery Babylon. We are seeing a progression of future history in these passages. Mystery Babylon, the first beast of Daniel 7 (the winged lion), will be destroyed by an axis of northern nations with Russia (the second bear beast of Daniel 7) at the helm. These nations will form the eventual core of the axis of nations that make up the fourth terrible beast of Daniel 7, which is the horned beast of Revelation 17. It is likely, given this progression, that the third leopard beast of Daniel 7 will also be one of the satellite nations of this axis.

In Revelation 17:18, the angel finally identifies the woman of John's vision; she is "that great city, which reigneth over the kings of the earth." At the time of her apex, the city and nation of Mystery Babylon will be a superpower with global influence.

Revelation 18 continues with details of the destruction of Mystery Babylon. An angelic messenger decries her crimes against God:

"And after these things I saw another angel come down from heaven, having great power; and the earth was lightened with his glory.

And he cried mightily with a strong voice, saying, Babylon the great is fallen, is fallen, and is become the habitation of devils, and the hold of every foul spirit, and a cage of every unclean and hateful bird.

For all nations have drunk of the wine of the wrath of her fornication, and the kings of the earth have committed fornication with her, and the merchants of the earth are waxed rich through the abundance of her delicacies.

And I heard another voice from heaven, saying, Come out of her, my people, that ye be not partakers of her sins, and that ye receive not of her plagues.

For her sins have reached unto heaven, and God hath remembered her iniquities.

Reward her even as she rewarded you, and double unto her double according to her works: in the cup which she hath filled fill to her double.

How much she hath glorified herself, and lived deliciously, so much torment and sorrow give her: for she saith in her heart, I sit a queen, and am no widow, and shall see no sorrow.

Therefore shall her plagues come in one day, death,

and mourning, and famine; and she shall be utterly burned with fire: for strong is the Lord God who judgeth her."

Revelation 18:1-8

How often the Scriptures speak of Mystery Babylon's destruction by fire and arrows! Her fall will be sudden and violent, and she will be left utterly desolate. Revelation 18:4 echoes the same warning that Jeremiah 50 and 51 repeat over and over: "Get out of Babylon, my people, lest you be destroyed in her judgment!" The presence of this warning in Revelation chapter 18 firmly links this passage to Jeremiah's Babylon and lends more clarity to Jeremiah's message. Revelation is a book written not only for Jews but for *all* of God's saints and true believers, Jew or Christian; Mystery Babylon will be a nation with a Christian population.

And why shall these things befall Babylon? Revelation 17 and 18 iterate her crimes again and again, lest they be overlooked: fornication (18:3), cruelty (18:6), hedonism and pride (18:7), materialism (18:14). Though Babylon may be a wonder to all the nations, she is guilty in the eyes of the God of Heaven, and worthy of judgment.

"And the kings of the earth, who have committed fornication and lived deliciously with her, shall bewail her, and lament for her, when they shall see the smoke of her burning,

"Standing afar off for the fear of her torment, saying, Alas, alas, that great city Babylon, that mighty

city! for in one hour is thy judgment come.

"And the merchants of the earth shall weep and mourn over her; for no man buyeth their merchandise any more:

"The merchandise of gold, and silver, and precious stones, and of pearls, and fine linen, and purple, and silk, and scarlet, and all thyine wood, and all manner vessels of ivory, and all manner vessels of most precious wood, and of brass, and iron, and marble,

"And cinnamon, and odours, and ointments, and frankincense, and wine, and oil, and fine flour, and wheat, and beasts, and sheep, and horses, and chariots, and slaves, and souls of men.

And the fruits that thy soul lusted after are departed from thee, and all things which were dainty and goodly are departed from thee, and thou shalt find them no more at all.

The merchants of these things, which were made rich by her, shall stand afar off for the fear of her torment, weeping and wailing,

And saying, Alas, alas, that great city, that was clothed in fine linen, and purple, and scarlet, and decked with gold, and precious stones, and pearls!

For in one hour so great riches is come to nought. And every shipmaster, and all the company in ships, and sailors, and as many as trade by sea, stood afar off,

And cried when they saw the smoke of her burning, saying, What city is like unto this great city!

And they cast dust on their heads, and cried, weeping and wailing, saying, Alas, alas, that great city, wherein were made rich all that had ships in the sea by reason of her costliness! for in one hour is she made desolate."

Revelation 18:9-19

We see from Revelation 18:9-19 that the fall of Mystery Babylon will shake the global economy to the core. As the primary first-world consumer nation of her time, her absence will leave a void in the international market that will stagger the fortunes of many. Babylon's downfall will be so sudden that the world could not have seen it coming; merchants already en route to her ports will anchor afar off, for fear that they will be caught up in her fiery destruction. Babylon's wealth, prestige, power, and international influence will not save her from the fire.

"Rejoice over her, thou heaven, and ye holy apostles and prophets; for God hath avenged you on her.

And a mighty angel took up a stone like a great millstone, and cast it into the sea, saying, Thus with violence shall that great city Babylon be thrown down, and shall be found no more at all.

And the voice of harpers, and musicians, and of pipers, and trumpeters, shall be heard no more at all in thee; and no craftsman, of whatsoever craft he be, shall be found any more in thee; and the sound of a millstone shall be heard no more at all in thee;

And the light of a candle shall shine no more at all in thee; and the voice of the bridegroom and of the bride shall be heard no more at all in thee: for thy merchants were the great men of the earth; for by thy sorceries were all nations deceived."

Revelation 18:20-23

Babylon, a city and a nation of industry, of music and culture, of craftsmanship, of shimmering lights, of celebration, will be silent and dark. Her financiers once ruled the global markets, but they will be gone. Her technology elevated her to a position of supremacy, but she will be cast down into darkness. Her bloodguiltiness before God will be fully judged:

"And in her was found the blood of prophets, and of saints, and of all that were slain upon the earth.

And after these things I heard a great voice of much people in heaven, saying, Alleluia; Salvation, and glory, and honour, and power, unto the Lord our God:

For true and righteous are his judgments: for he hath judged the great whore, which did corrupt the earth with her fornication, and hath avenged the blood of his servants at her hand.

And again they said, Alleluia. And her smoke rose up for ever and ever."

Revelation 18:24-19:3

Consider for a moment all the things that God says in His Word about Mystery Babylon, and all the things that the people of the earth say about her. While the people of the nations laud and admire Babylon, and run to her and emulate her, God condemns her. We see that God's perspective and values are very different from that of humanity.

I don't think the topic of the next chapter will be a great surprise. I suspect the title of this book and the things we have already discussed have made the inevitable conclusion clear. In the next chapter we will look at all of the Biblical prophecies that show quite conclusively that the United States of America is indeed the identity of Mystery Babylon. I encourage you to approach that chapter with an open mind and an open Bible. Consider prayerfully whether these things are true.

"The Lord is not slack concerning his promise, as some men count slackness; but is longsuffering to us-ward, not willing that any should perish, but that all should come to repentance."

2 Peter 3:9

Chapter 5:
America Is Mystery Babylon

Isaiah 47, Jeremiah 50 and 51, Revelation 16:19-19:3

~

"He answered and said unto them, When it is evening, ye say, It will be fair weather: for the sky is red.

And in the morning, It will be foul weather to day: for the sky is red and lowring. O ye hypocrites, ye can discern the face of the sky; but can ye not discern the signs of the times?"

Matthew 16:2-3

These passages in Isaiah, Jeremiah, and Revelation depict modern America.

I hope that it is clear from what we have considered thus far that the sections of Scripture concerning the fall of Babylon cannot be portrayals of the fall of the ancient Neo-Babylonian Empire. We can also draw two further conclusions with certainty: (1) these chapters all concern the prophesied destruction of the same entity, Mystery Babylon, and (2) at the time that these portions of the Bible were written, Mystery Babylon was a future kingdom which did not then exist.

We can logically arrive at that first conclusion based on the remarkable parallelism of Jeremiah 50 and 51, Revelation 16-19, and Isaiah 47 (which we have not yet explored in detail, but which we will visit later):

- All three of these books of the Bible mention destruction by fire.
- The physical descriptions in these passages of a decadent world power are the same.
- Mystery Babylon, personified, describes herself with similar language in these passages: "I am a lady," "I shall never be a widow," "I shall never know loss of children," etc.
- All three of these books have the same sins associated with Mystery Babylon: pride, sexual wickedness, materialism, etc.
- In all three passages, Mystery Babylon relies on her sorceries and advisors to save her from destruction, but they are unable to do so.
- All three passages describe passers-by seeing the destruction of Mystery Babylon and the unsettling effect that destruction has on the nations of the world.

These specific details link these passages and make it apparent that these prophecies concern the same events. This interconnectedness of these three Bible passages also leads us towards our second conclusion concerning the timing of Mystery Babylon's reign; Mystery Babylon could not have been ancient Babylon since it must be, according to John's vision in Revelation, a future nation which had not yet then arisen. The book of Revelation, when compared with Daniel 7, makes it clear that Mystery Babylon is an end times nation which is seperate from the Antichrist's kingdom and which will precede it.

These two conclusions eliminate a great many possibilities, and we are left to consider Mystery Babylon's identity based upon the numerous detailed descriptions of her in Isaiah, Jeremiah, and Revelation. This exploration is the purpose of this chapter, and we will see, piece by piece, that Mystery Babylon must be the United States of America. This is a difficult thing for you to hear, I am sure, and as I have mentioned, a difficult thing for me to write about, in some ways. But if it is the truth, we must not shy away from it; we must face it with an open mind and consider what these things will mean for us.

Mystery Babylon is portrayed as a prostitute in Scripture.

Many Americans are unaware of the deeper significance of the Statue of Liberty, one of the predominant icons of the United States of America. This sculpture, designed by the Frenchman Frederic

Auguste Bartholdi, is actually titled "Liberty Enlightening the World." Bartholdi, a sculptor obsessed with collossal statuary, authored a little book titled, "The Statue of Liberty enlightening the world" (actual capitalization) in English, which I have as a digital scan. The formatting of the booklet, with "The Statue of Liberty" being capitalized and prominently displayed above the lowercase "enlightening the world" doubtless helped to contribute to our modern colloquial nomenclature of the piece as simply "The Statue of Liberty." While Bartholdi was the actual sculptor of the Statue of Liberty, he was influenced in his subject selection by a fellow named Edward Laboulaye, a French Freemason who raised funding and support for the project, and who delivered a rousing speech when the statue was actually given to America by France.

"Liberty Enlightening the World" is a depiction of the Roman goddess of liberty, Libertas. While originally Libertas had an association with the general concept of freedom, in the ancient world that connotation evolved to mean something quite different. Under the Romans, many freed slaves chose Libertas as their personal patron deity given their newly emancipated state. While some slaves were able to find an occupation and provide for themselves, those of lower social class, education, and skill often resorted to prostitution, especially ritual prostitution associated with many of the temples of Roman deities, in order to sustain themselves. The association of

Libertas with these shrine prostitutes eventually resulted in the goddess assuming a different meaning; Libertas became the patron goddess of... sexual liberty.

I have not studied any primary source documents concerning this topic for myself, but I will make mention that many scholars trace the origins of Libertas back in history even further to a mother-goddess precursor. These scholars suggest that many ancient deities were borrowed from this "Queen of Heaven": Venus, Aphrodite, Astarte, Ashtoreh, Isis, and Ishtar, amongst others. The differences between these derivative goddesses come from their followers' preference for certain of the goddesses' traits over others. Many of these goddesses' temple cults had a striking commonality: an emphasis upon ritual sex as a means of spiritual "purification." Many of these goddesses are also associated with the moon, and Belshazzar may have been toasting Babylon's version of the "Queen of Heaven" during the ill-fated feast on the night that ancient Babylon fell to the Medes and Persians (Daniel 5).

I doubt most Americans think of Lady Liberty in these terms, but the ancient stigma remains a historical fact. How exactly is Liberty "enlightening the world"? The sculpture's official title is thought provoking in light of Scripture's accusation that Babylon has made all the nations of the earth to drink of the wine of the wrath of her fornication. We will discuss Mystery Babylon's sexual wickedness in more detail in a subsequent section of this chapter.

I will briefly make mention of the most widespread interpretation of the identity of Mystery Babylon today, because it relates to the portrayal of this nation as the Whore of Babylon. It has long been speculated that Mystery Babylon might be the Catholic church. This speculation was the logical extension of the religious upheaval surrounding the Protestant Reformations; the Roman Catholic Church was a powerful political entity at the time and it sought to suppress views which it did not endorse and to keep the Bible out of the hands of the common people. The connection between the unfaithful Whore of Babylon and the spiritual unfaithfulness of the Roman Church was therefore a logical one... for Protestants during that period of time. But we can see clearly now that this explanation simply does not hold up under scrutinty of the Biblical prophecies or in light of the development of history since the Reformation. The Roman Catholic Church, while still doctrinally and morally corrupt, is simply no longer a powerful entity holding sway over the kings of the earth, nor is it a consumerist nation.

Mystery Babylon is both a city and a nation.

Revelation describes Mystery Babylon as both a nation and a "great city":

"And the great city was divided into three parts, and the cities of the nations fell: and great Babylon came

in remembrance before God, to give unto her the cup of the wine of the fierceness of his wrath."
Revelation 16:19

New York City, the home of the Statue of Liberty, is one of the greatest metropoles in humanity's history. America's most populous city, New York City is situated at the site of one of the world's largest natural harbors, and its greater metropolitan area has tens of millions of residents. The great city is indeed divided into three parts geographically: the three islands (Manhattan, Staten, and Long Islands) upon which it is situated. New York City's five boroughs are each virtually a distinct and diverse city unto itself. (Interestingly, Babylon is also the name of a district almost exactly in the middle of New York's Long Island.)

New York City has been called the "capital of the world," and Wall Street is the heart of the world's financial infrastructure. The city is a major shipping and commerce hub; New York Harbor accomodates more tonnage of goods than any other port on the East Coast, and it is the third largest harbor in the United States by tonnage. New York City is also a major world cultural center, home to many communities of artists, filmmakers, and musicians.

Mystery Babylon is situated on many waters.

In Revelation 17:1, the very first thing which

the angel mentions to the apostle John about Mystery Babylon is that "the great whore ... sitteth upon many waters." Babylon's association with seas and waters is mentioned in both Jeremiah and Revelation:

*"A drought is upon **her waters**; and they shall be dried up: for it is the land of graven images, and they are mad upon their idols."*
Jeremiah 50:38

*"O thou that **dwellest upon many waters**, abundant in treasures, thine end is come, and the measure of thy covetousness."*
Jeremiah 51:13

*"Therefore thus saith the LORD; Behold, I will plead thy cause, and take vengeance for thee; and I will dry up **her sea**, and make her **springs dry**."*
Jeremiah 51:36

*"**The sea is come up upon Babylon**: she is covered with the multitude of the waves thereof."*
Jeremiah 51:42

*"For in one hour so great riches is come to nought. And every **shipmaster, and all the company in ships, and sailors, and as many as trade by sea**, stood afar off,*

*And cried when they saw the smoke of her burning, saying, What **city** is like unto this **great city**!*

And they cast dust on their heads, and cried, weeping and wailing, saying, Alas, alas, that ***great city****, wherein were made rich* ***all that had ships in the sea*** *by reason of her costliness! for in one hour is she made desolate."*

Revelation 18:17-19

Most of the language of these Bible verses is quite literal; both the nation and the city of Mystery Babylon are situated near or upon many waters. New York City was built upon a natural harbor where the Hudson River flows into the Atlantic Ocean. The United States of America has plentiful waterways, from the Great Lakes, which are seas in themselves, to the mighty Mississippi River, the wide artery of trade in the very heart of the continent, to the Gulf of Mexico, not to mention the Atlantic and Pacific Oceans as well. According to the National Oceanic and Atmospheric Administration (NOAA), America has over 95,000 miles of shoreline, both along fresh and salt water bodies. I would be remiss to overlook something which the angel in Revelation 17 specifically mentions to the apostle John, which is that the waters upon which Babylon sits are both literal *and* symbolic. These waters represent the diversity of the nations and peoples who live within Mystery Babylon (which we will discuss in the next section):

"And he saith unto me, The waters which thou sawest, where the whore sitteth, are peoples, and

multitudes, and nations, and tongues."
Revelation 17:15

Mystery Babylon is a culturally diverse nation, full of immigrants, refugees, alien workers, and citizens of various ethnic backgrounds.

The prosperity of America has caused people to "flow into her" from nearly every corner of the world. Historically these diverse peoples lived and worked within the United States of America and many even became American citizens themselves; this is the source of America's great "melting pot" of diversity and cultural richness. Sadly, many of these people will be killed or forced to flee when Mystery Babylon's destruction falls:

"Thus shall they be unto thee with whom thou hast laboured, even thy merchants, from thy youth: ***they shall wander every one to his quarter****; none shall save thee."*
Isaiah 47:15

"A sword is upon their horses, and upon their chariots, and upon all the ***mingled people that are in the midst of her****; and they shall become as women: a sword is upon her treasures; and they shall be robbed."*
Jeremiah 50:37

"As Babylon hath caused the slain of Israel to fall,

so ***at Babylon shall fall the slain of all the earth**."*
Jeremiah 51:49

"Cut off the sower from Babylon, and him that handleth the sickle in the time of harvest: for fear of the oppressing sword ***they shall turn every one to his people, and they shall flee every one to his own land**."*
Jeremiah 50:16

"Thus saith the LORD; Behold, I will raise up against Babylon, and ***against them that dwell in the midst of them that rise up against me**, a destroying wind;"*
Jeremiah 51:1

"We would have healed Babylon, but she is not healed: forsake her, and ***let us go every one into his own country**: for her judgment reacheth unto heaven, and is lifted up even to the skies."*
Jeremiah 51:9

"And I will punish Bel in Babylon, and ***I will bring forth out of his mouth that which he hath swallowed up**: and* ***the nations shall not flow together any more unto him**: yea, the wall of Babylon shall fall."*
Jeremiah 51:44

Look at the tremendous specificity of these

Bible verses. Isaiah 47:15 mentions all those who have come to America because it is a prosperous place to live and work. Jeremiah 50:16 describes seasonal migrant agricultural workers, upon whose labor the fruit industry of the American West Coast depends. Jeremiah 51:9 shows that these people love America and would build her back up if only they could, but her destruction is too complete and they will be forced to flee. Sadly, many will be unable to flee and so the slain of the whole earth will fall in Babylon.

Mystery Babylon is a materialistic, wealthy, consumerist nation.

The Scriptures make it plain that Mystery Babylon, like modern America, is the world's greatest consumer nation during the time of her apex. Her destruction will be greatly mourned by the world's merchants and exporters:

"And the merchants of the earth shall weep and mourn over her; for no man buyeth their merchandise any more:

The merchandise of gold, and silver, and precious stones, and of pearls, and fine linen, and purple, and silk, and scarlet, and all thyine wood, and all manner vessels of ivory, and all manner vessels of most precious wood, and of brass, and iron, and marble,

And cinnamon, and odours, and ointments, and frankincense, and wine, and oil, and fine flour, and wheat, and beasts, and sheep, and horses, and chariots, and slaves, and souls of men.

And the fruits that thy soul lusted after are departed from thee, and all things which were dainty and goodly are departed from thee, and thou shalt find them no more at all.

The merchants of these things, which were made rich by her, shall stand afar off for the fear of her torment, weeping and wailing,

And saying, Alas, alas, that great city, that was clothed in fine linen, and purple, and scarlet, and decked with gold, and precious stones, and pearls!

For in one hour so great riches is come to nought. And every shipmaster, and all the company in ships, and sailors, and as many as trade by sea, stood afar off,

And cried when they saw the smoke of her burning, saying, What city is like unto this great city!

And they cast dust on their heads, and cried, weeping and wailing, saying, Alas, alas, that great city, wherein were made rich all that had ships in the sea by reason of her costliness! for in one hour is she made desolate."

Revelation 18:11-19

America is the wealthiest nation which has ever existed in modern history. The average American citizen has a safer food and water supply and eats more luxuriously than any king of ancient times; modern technology ensures the freshness, variety, and availability of a plethora of fruits and vegetables even when these are not in season. In the ancient world, entire families often lived in houses with only one or two rooms, or even in tents for those who were less settled. For a child who was not nobility to have their own bedroom was nearly unheard of in ancient times. A horse was a luxury that few common folk could afford to purchase or upkeep; how many modern American families today have multiple automobiles? Only the greatest and most advanced cities of antiquity had running water; the majority of Americans have access to running water, electricity, and all the benefits these utilities afford. The wealth of the average American is also astounding, even compared to other nations in the modern world. No other nation's citizens have such a large percentage of disposable income as Americans do.

There is nothing inherently wrong with material wealth or comforts. But instead of America's blessings making her more prudent and thankful, Americans have become over time more arrogant, wasteful, greedy, materialistic, and entitled. The covetousness of Mystery Babylon is one of the cardinal sins for which God will judge her:

"O thou that dwellest upon many waters, abundant in treasures, thine end is come, and the measure of thy covetousness."

Jeremiah 51:13

Mystery Babylon is a nation of wanton idolatry.

It might be strange to think of America as being "idolatrous." Modern American society is increasingly secularized and not particularly superstitious, at least not compared to many other nations which still do actively practice idolatry, such as many nations in East Asia. Mystery Babylon will be a nation of rampant, mad idolatry:

"Declare ye among the nations, and publish, and set up a standard; publish, and conceal not: say, Babylon is taken, Bel is confounded, Merodach is broken in pieces; her idols are confounded, her images are broken in pieces."
Jeremiah 50:2

"A drought is upon her waters; and they shall be dried up: for it is the land of graven images, and they are mad upon their idols."
Jeremiah 50:38

The idolatrous tendencies of the human heart are still present in modern America. Human beings have a need to worship, and if the object of their worship is not the God of Heaven, it is an idolatrous worship. America knows that ancient pagan deities of stone and metal are useless and foolish, but there are other far more exciting and insidious gods to worship in modern American society than the deities of the ancient past.

America worships the various gods of leisure and culture: professional sports athletes, musicians (tellingly described as "pop idols"), actors and entertainers, the worlds of fantasy and video games. Summer blockbuster movies make hundreds of millions of dollars in a single weekend; sports teams are valued at tens or hundreds of millions of dollars; superstar athletes sign contracts for fortunes. Paparazzi and fans obsess over their favorite actors, musicians, Youtube personalities, and sports figures. Both the music and movie industries in America are worth tens of billions of dollars. America's appetite for experiences and heroes is bottomless. America is "mad upon her idols," and sadly the general American populace emulates the wanton, dissipated, sexually lascivious, materialistic, violent, arrogant lifestyle of her clay-footed gods.

Mystery Babylon has a mother country.

Jeremiah 50 verse 12 says (to Mystery Babylon), "Your mother shall be sore confounded; she that bare you shall be ashamed." Many nations cannot claim a clear "mother country," but America can. The United States of America is a former colony of Great Britain, and we still resemble our mother country greatly in terms of culture, language, and ideology.

Mystery Babylon will have a large population of Jews.

The Diaspora, or scattering of the Jewish people throughout the nations of the world, was a judgment upon them by God for the Jews' forsaking His laws. Isaiah 47:6 specifically mentions those scattered Jews which are living within Mystery Babylon:

"I was wroth with my people, I have polluted mine inheritance, and given them into thine hand: thou didst shew them no mercy; upon the ancient hast thou very heavily laid thy yoke."
Isaiah 47:6

This language seems harsh and perhaps out of place if one is considering these words in relation to Jews living in America. Can it really be said of these Jews that they have been polluted? I believe so. A large portion of the Jews living in the United States are very critical, even hateful, towards the state of Israel. "Pollution" can have many connotations; it is reminiscent of God's warnings to His people not to intermix their bloodlines with those of their heathen neighbors in the Old Testament, and could possibly relate to the dilution of Jewish culture, or the corrupting of the purity of God's law by living amongst a foreign nation with very different moral standards.

One of God's purposes in the judgment of Mystery Babylon will be to return the very large Jewish population living there to Israel. It is interesting to note that these refugee Jews weep over their former home as they return to their ancestral homeland:

"In those days, and in that time, saith the LORD, the children of Israel shall come, they and the children of Judah together, going and weeping: they shall go, and seek the LORD their God.

They shall ask the way to Zion with their faces thitherward, saying, Come, and let us join ourselves to the LORD in a perpetual covenant that shall not be forgotten."

Jeremiah 50:4-5

"And I will bring Israel again to his habitation, and he shall feed on Carmel and Bashan, and his soul shall be satisfied upon mount Ephraim and Gilead.

In those days, and in that time, saith the LORD, the iniquity of Israel shall be sought for, and there shall be none; and the sins of Judah, and they shall not be found: for I will pardon them whom I reserve."

Jeremiah 50:19-20

The presence of these Jews in Mystery Babylon is extremely significant. While a very small handful of nations have Jewish populations numbering in the hundreds of thousands, there are *only two nations* with Jewish populations numbering in the millions: Israel... and the United States of America. The fall of Mystery Babylon will motivate these exiled American Jews to return to their nation and their God:

"The voice of them that flee and escape out of the land of Babylon, to declare in Zion the vengeance of the LORD our God, the vengeance of his temple."

Jeremiah 50:28

"Their [the Jews'] Redeemer is strong; the LORD of hosts is his name: he shall throughly plead their cause, that he may give rest to the land [of Israel], and disquiet the inhabitants of Babylon."
Jeremiah 50:34

Mystery Babylon will have a large population of Christians.

"We are confounded, because we have heard reproach: shame hath covered our faces: for strangers are come into the sanctuaries of the LORD'S house."
Jeremiah 51:51

This is an interesting verse in Jeremiah; to my knowledge the Jews historically recognized only *one* sanctuary, the Jewish temple, so considering this verse in light of Revelation 18:4 (see the next section), which was written to Christians and which warns God's people to flee out of Babylon, the Scriptures seem to strongly indicate that Mystery Babylon will also have a large population of Christians. These Christians will be dismayed and distressed when destruction overtakes the true churches of Mystery Babylon. The United States of America is predominantly "Christian" with over 70% of the population identifying with various Protestant denominations or with Roman Catholicism. Of course, the percentage of true, Bible-believing Christians is much, much lower, but there are still hundreds of true

Christian churches and perhaps millions of true Christian believers living in America today.

God's people (Jews and Christians) living in Mystery Babylon are free to leave of their own volition.

The warnings of God prompted me to write this book. The three-fold repetition of Jeremiah chapters 50 and 51 caught my attention as I read that passage, and when I realized that Revelation chapter 18 contained a similar command of God to flee Mystery Babylon, I realized that these two passages of Scripture were linked and portended the same events. Read these warnings carefully for yourself:

"Remove out of the midst of Babylon, and go forth out of the land of the Chaldeans, and be as the he goats before the flocks."
Jeremiah 50:8

"Flee out of the midst of Babylon, and deliver every man his soul: be not cut off in her iniquity; for this is the time of the LORD'S vengeance; he will render unto her a recompence."
Jeremiah 51:6

"My people, go ye out of the midst of her, and deliver ye every man his soul from the fierce

anger of the LORD."
Jeremiah 51:45

"And I heard another voice from heaven, saying, Come out of her, my people, that ye be not partakers of her sins, and that ye receive not of her plagues."
Revelation 18:4

Notice the implications of these warnings. Destruction is nearly certain for those who choose to stay in Babylon. The word "soul" in Jeremiah is a bit of an archaic usage of the word, which originally was taken to mean simply "life" or "person." This is clearly not merely a metaphorical or spiritual destruction that will overtake Mystery Babylon; it is a real, physical destruction and God's people are meant to pay attention to these warnings and act upon them, for in so doing they may be able to save their lives from the coming destruction!

Notice also that these commands require that God's people living in Mystery Babylon must be free persons possessing the self-determination to obey these commands of God. These warnings are obviously not in reference to ancient Babylon, for the Hebrew slaves could not simply come or go as they pleased. This is a warning for God's people living in America today. Do not be caught up in God's judgment of wicked Babylon when it comes! Flee and save yourselves alive!

These are hard sayings, and it will require faith for God's people to act. God gives us a sign in the Scriptures about when the time will be right to leave Mystery Babylon, and we will discuss this sign in detail in a later chapter:

"And lest your heart faint, and ye fear for the rumour that shall be heard in the land; a rumour shall both come one year, and after that in another year shall come a rumour, and violence in the land, ruler against ruler.

Therefore, behold, the days come, that I will do judgment upon the graven images of Babylon: and her whole land shall be confounded, and all her slain shall fall in the midst of her."

Jeremiah 51:46-47

Mystery Babylon is technologically advanced.

"Stand now with thine enchantments, and with the multitude of thy sorceries, wherein thou hast laboured from thy youth; if so be thou shalt be able to profit, if so be thou mayest prevail.

Thou art wearied in the multitude of thy counsels. Let now the astrologers, the stargazers, the monthly prognosticators, stand up, and save thee from these things that shall come upon thee."

Isaiah 47:12-13

The language here is a bit archaic, but it is clear that Mystery Babylon will be a nation of high technology. Our understandings of technology, wisdom, and science have changed greatly since the book of Isaiah was penned, but the description does not go amiss. America is a land of scientific and technological marvels; we have a plethora of learned experts, great innovaters, brilliant scientists, studied historians, and plenty of hard-working, enterprising individuals. But God warns that no technological solution or grand strategy will save Mystery Babylon from the fires of His divine judgment.

Mystery Babylon has mounted up to the heavens.

"Though Babylon should mount up to heaven, and though she should fortify the height of her strength, yet from me shall spoilers come unto her, saith the LORD."
Jeremiah 51:53

There are several ways to approach this verse, and I will present all three instead of dogmatically adhering to any one explanation, since all three are true of America. Some commentators suggest that this verse means Mystery Babylon will be a first-world nation capable of space flight and space exploration. Certainly America and American industry have been and remain the forerunners of innovation pertaining to outer space travel. Others have suggested that this verse refers to air superiority (especially in light of the verse's connotation of military strength) and normal flight capability: airplanes and warplanes. America has the best fighter planes and supporting infrastructure of any nation, and in any theater of conflict, American air power dominates the airspace without question. Yet another more traditional explanation of this verse is simply that Mystery Babylon is arrogant and elevates herself in her arrogant pride above all others. This description would fit the United States of America as well.

I see no reason to arbitrarily pick one of these explanations, especially since all of them are appropriate. One of them is surely the original intended meaning, and it remains a true assessment; America has indeed "mounted up to heaven" in more ways than one.

Mystery Babylon is a sexually immoral nation and the origin of the sexual revolution.

America is the only nation that fits this description. *The United States of America produces more than two-thirds of all pornographic material.* Yes, you read that statistic correctly. It was here in the United States of America that the sexual revolution and the concept of "free love" caught fire in the 1960s and spread to all the nations of the modern era:

"Babylon hath been a golden cup in the LORD'S hand, that made all the earth drunken: the nations have

drunken of her wine; therefore the nations are mad."
Jeremiah 51:7

"With whom the kings of the earth have committed fornication, and the inhabitants of the earth have been made drunk with the wine of her fornication."
Revelation 17:2

No wonder Mystery Babylon is described as the Mother of Harlots, and is depicted as a prostitute intoxicated by the contents of her golden cup full of immorality:

"And the woman was arrayed in purple and scarlet colour, and decked with gold and precious stones and pearls, having a golden cup in her hand full of abominations and filthiness of her fornication:
And upon her forehead was a name written, MYSTERY, BABYLON THE GREAT, THE MOTHER OF HARLOTS AND ABOMINATIONS OF THE EARTH."
Revelation 17:4-5

Mystery Babylon is a hedonistic nation.

This may be an entirely redundant observation at this point. There is so much overlap in the wickednesses of Mystery Babylon: riotous living, drunkenness, sexual immorality. We have already seen Bible verses describing all these sins, but here are a few more to further emphasize the point that Mystery

Babylon embraces hedonism as a pervasive lifestyle. None of these things are unfamiliar to modern American society:

"In their heat ***I will make their feasts, and I will make them drunken, that they may rejoice****, and sleep a perpetual sleep, and not wake, saith the LORD."*

Jeremiah 51:39

"For all nations have drunk of the wine of the wrath of ***her fornication****, and* ***the kings of the earth have committed fornication with her****, and the merchants of the earth are waxed rich through the* ***abundance of her delicacies****."*

Revelation 18:3

"How much ***she hath glorified herself, and lived deliciously****, so much torment and sorrow give her: for she saith in her heart, I sit a queen, and am no widow, and shall see no sorrow."*

Revelation 18:7

"Therefore hear now this, ***thou that art given to pleasures, that dwellest carelessly****, that sayest in thine heart, I am, and none else beside me; I shall not sit as a widow, neither shall I know the loss of children:*

But these two things shall come to thee in a moment in one day, the loss of children, and widowhood: they shall come upon thee in their perfection for ***the***

multitude of thy sorceries, and for the great abundance of thine enchantments.

For ***thou hast trusted in thy wickedness: thou hast said, None seeth me****. Thy wisdom and thy knowledge, it hath perverted thee; and thou hast said in thine heart, I am, and none else beside me.*

Therefore shall evil come upon thee; thou shalt not know from whence it riseth: and mischief shall fall upon thee; thou shalt not be able to put it off: and desolation shall come upon thee suddenly, which thou shalt not know."

Isaiah 47:8-11

Mystery Babylon is a powerful, militaristic nation.

Mystery Babylon is depicted as a powerful conquering nation. Jeremiah 50 and 51 mention men of war, bows, horses, chariots, strong walls, and high gates over and over again. The Scriptures tell us that her judgment by God is partly a recompense for things that Mystery Babylon has done to other nations; her judgment is partly a physical consequence of her own military aggression. God also describes Mystery Babylon as His "battleaxe" and "the hammer of the whole earth," a tool with which He casts down nations according to His will:

"How is the hammer of the whole earth cut asunder and broken! how is Babylon become a desolation

among the nations!"
Jeremiah 50:23

"Thou art my battle axe and weapons of war: for with thee will I break in pieces the nations, and with thee will I destroy kingdoms;

And with thee will I break in pieces the horse and his rider; and with thee will I break in pieces the chariot and his rider;

With thee also will I break in pieces man and woman; and with thee will I break in pieces old and young; and with thee will I break in pieces the young man and the maid;

I will also break in pieces with thee the shepherd and his flock; and with thee will I break in pieces the husbandman and his yoke of oxen; and with thee will I break in pieces captains and rulers."
Jeremiah 51:20-23

As I contemplate these verses' description of a mighty world power dominating lesser nations and crushing shepherds, farmers, kings, and generals, I cannot help but picture in my mind's eye scenes from America's countless foreign wars and interventions: the Tripolitan Wars, the Cuban-American War, both World Wars, Korea, Vietnam, the Gulf War, Iraq, Afghanistan, and dozens of others besides. American troops have been part of numerous coalitions and international peacekeeping forces as well; America has been militarily active on every populated continent. America has been in a constant state of war for my entire life. America has been at war continuously for most (if not all) of the last century.

A tragic side effect of any war, even the most just conflict, is collateral damage and loss of innocent life. In the Iraq war alone, there have been over 100,000 confirmed innocent civilian casualties, and some sources say that number is actually nearly double that figure. This statistic represents one rather asymmetrical war, in one country.

The sad truth is that America's wars have often *not* been just wars. There are several conflicts in which America should not have gotten involved in the first place, and many American soldiers who fought (often unwillingly) in those conflicts are ashamed to this day to admit that they served in those wars. The history of American war is a history fraught with bungling and incompetence at the highest levels of command, and senseless politics resulting in massive losses of life, civilian lives, foreign lives, lives of American patriots. As the Scriptures say of Mystery Babylon, much of America's time in several of these foreign wars has been spent fighting ragtag armies of improvised soldiers who were erstwhile farmers, shepherds, and peasants.

America idolizes its soldiers and those who support them, and the nation is willing to overlook a great deal of corruption surrounding the military and associated groups. I remember a decade ago the popular charity "Wounded Warrior Project" was given a "D" rating by a watchdog group because over 70% of donations given to the fund went to those who were administering it, in the form of six-figure salaries and other perks. Such abuses are hardly uncommon.

At the end of the day, the question also must be asked, who is guiding America's military decision making? Often there is no clear answer, and no justifiable reason for the conflicts in which America entangles itself. President George Bush led us into two wars after the 9/11 terrorist attacks on New York City, but during the summer of 2016, 28 previously classified pages of the 9/11 Commission's report were released to the public, pages which established ties between the 9/11 hijackers and Saudi Arabian intelligence. Was the "War on Terror" even fought against the right adversaries? America often goes to war without clear objectives, and finishes without a clear victory or real progress. Many of America's bitterest foes were created by America herself.

"Call together the archers against Babylon: all ye that bend the bow, camp against it round about; let none thereof escape: ***recompense her according to her work; according to all that she hath done, do unto her****: for she hath been proud against the LORD, against the Holy One of Israel.*

Therefore shall her young men fall in the streets, and all her men of war shall be cut off in that day, saith the LORD.

Behold, I am against thee, O thou most proud, saith the Lord GOD of hosts: for thy day is come, the time that I will visit thee.

And the most proud shall stumble and fall, and none shall raise him up: and I will kindle a fire in his cities, and it shall devour all round about him."

Jeremiah 50:29-32

"Behold, I am against thee, ***O destroying mountain****, saith the LORD,* ***which destroyest all the earth****: and I will stretch out mine hand upon thee, and roll thee down from the rocks, and will make thee a burnt mountain."*

Jeremiah 51:25

Mystery Babylon's fall will shake the entire world.

Imagine what would happen if America instantly disappeared right now. The American dollar would immediately be worthless; those nations and persons who have chosen to store their wealth in American currencies or securities would lose those investments. Nations which have built their entire economies around trade and export with the United States would be economically crippled. Nations which rely on the hundreds of millions of dollars of foreign aid that America once pumped out now cannot rely on that financial lifeline. America's allies who depend upon the United States to secure them from the aggression of ambitious neighbors will suddenly have little or no defense. Ravenous great nations that the

United States has long held in check with the threat of military might will greedily expand to fill the new power vacuum. The world will be utterly shaken; some nations will cease to exist, others will rise, others will be plunged into extreme poverty. We see all these things in Scripture; when Mystery Babylon falls, the world will be an entirely different place:

"At the noise of the taking of Babylon the earth is moved, and the cry is heard among the nations."
Jeremiah 50:46

"And the kings of the earth, who have committed fornication and lived deliciously with her, shall bewail her, and lament for her, when they shall see the smoke of her burning."
Revelation 18:9

"How is Sheshach taken! and how is the praise of the whole earth surprised! how is Babylon become an astonishment among the nations!"
Jeremiah 51:41

"Then the heaven and the earth, and all that is therein, shall sing for Babylon: for the spoilers shall come unto her from the north, saith the LORD."
Jeremiah 51:48

An Unpleasant But Obvious Conclusion

Perhaps you have heard of the principle of

Occam's Razor. Occam's Razor is a tautology; it cannot be proven to be true, but it is considered to be true both because it is useful and because observationally it seems to be true in most situations. Occam's Razor states that given multiple explanations to the same question, the simplest explanation is most likely to be the true explanation.

Since I am an American, and a very old-fashioned patriotic, nationalistic one at that, it is very difficult for me to consider that my beloved homeland, the United States of America, could be the Mystery Babylon which will be judged by God in the future. But the Scriptures are very descriptive concerning Mystery Babylon, and it is time to move beyond our fixation upon those things we *wish* to be true, and try to find the actual truth with open mind. What is the simplest answer? Let us apply Occam's Razor.

Given the premises that

(A) The Biblical prophecies are accurate and true, and

(B) America fits the Biblical description of Mystery Babylon to an uncanny degree,

One of the following possibilities must be true:

(1) America is indeed Mystery Babylon and will fulfill the Biblical prophecies, or

(2) America is *not* Mystery Babylon, but will be replaced by another nation which will

become Mystery Babylon and *then* fulfill the

Biblical prophecies.

In either case America's dominance over the nations of the earth is fated to come to an end, but it is clear that conclusion (1), that America is indeed Mystery Babylon, is the simplest and most reasonable conclusion given what we know from Biblical prophecy. I have been very careful to be straightforward in my presentation of these things and to not misrepresent God's Word. I think if you are truly open-minded about these things, you will see the truth of it for yourself.

This is not what I would have wished or hoped for, but life is not a fairy tale. Human history is a long, sad accounting of how human wickedness and rebellion against God's truth leads to death, decay, destruction, and despair. Sadly there will be much more death, decay, destruction, and despair before God settles all accounts.

"Many shall be purified, and made white, and tried; but the wicked shall do wickedly: and none of the wicked shall understand; but the wise shall understand."
Daniel 12:10

Chapter 6:
America's Crimes Before God

Isaiah 47, Jeremiah 50 and 51,
Revelation 16:19-19:3

~

"It is an abomination to kings to commit wickedness: for the throne is established by righteousness."
Proverbs 16:12

America Is Not the Good Guy

I am sure that some of you may have some serious objections after reading the last chapter. "But J., America is a force for *good* in the world! We take out terrorists and other bad guys; we donate millions of dollars' worth of food aid and medical supplies; American volunteers provide medical services and disaster relief! And there are millions of ordinary, hard-working people living in America, even people of faith! How can America be Mystery Babylon?"

I once wrote a letter to the editor of a local newspaper in which I noted the vast gulf between America the ideal and America the reality. Americans do like to believe that America is a shining city on a hill and a force for good in the world, and indeed all true Americans should pursue that ideal. We love America because she represents human rights to "life, liberty, and the pursuit of happiness," and "liberty and justice for all" regardless of social status, ethnic background, religion, gender, or any other distinction. But at the same time that they love her, those Americans who are most awake and attentive realize that the reality of the United States of America is actually very different from the lofty ideals towards which we aspire. America, in reality, *is* a land of injustice, inequality, senseless violence, poverty, sickness, political corruption, and a great many other ills despite our best intentions.

Our adamant belief that America is a force for good is also colored by the reality that America *has been* a force for good *for Americans*. Americans live very secure, privileged lives, unlike most of those people born in other nations or in other periods of history. The freedom to speak, worship, or even think as one wishes are relatively new and radical phenomena on the stage of world events. We take these for granted, and we often don't realize that many of these blessings exist for us at the expense of others.

Many nations around the world do not see America as the "good guy," but as an oppressor. America has made herself the "policeman of the world," but the world has not asked America to police them. Indeed, America polices the world for her own sake, not for theirs. The United States of America intervenes in the destiny of nations because the USA wants a stable international environment where *America* can thrive. Sometimes America's efforts to forcibly enact her vision go amiss, and she instead creates more enemies for herself. A friend of mine recently visited several nations in southeast Asia. He and his American compatriots were not well-liked there due to many of America's botched interactions with countries in the region; in Vietnam, for example, the Vietnam War is known as "The War of American Aggression." My friend recounted how during one particular tour, the local tour guide struggled awkwardly to moderate his usual very anti-American commentary for his audience of American tourists. The Vietnam War was a war fought on behalf of European imperialism; America had no business intervening there.

America has often chosen to support dictators and regimes who have enacted genocides and ethnic purges. You may recall from your high school history classes that Soviet Russia was not an ally of the Allied Powers at the outset of World War II; Hitler's betrayal of his alliance with Russia resulted in the Russians joining the Allies against Hitler's Third Reich. But Russia's leader Joseph Stalin was every bit as cruel and murderous as the mad Adolf Hitler, and millions of innocents died under Stalin's regime. Some prominent Americans, including General Patton, felt that the Russians were barbarians and that US forces, upon taking Berlin, should have turned against the Russians and continued pushing east to Moscow. History might have been vastly different if Patton had enacted this vision; instead he died under suspicious circumstances in Europe and the Russian hordes raped millions of German women upon the fall of East Berlin, a scene rivaling the barbarism of the most violent sackings of ancient cities. After the war, Russia would be largely appeased by American leadership who were largely enamored by Stalin's charisma.

We could go on and on. We could discuss how America supported genocide in East Timor, a Pacific island nation that few Americans have even heard about. We could mention how American interference in Iran made that nation into the bitter enemy of America that she is today. We could discuss how American schemes created terrorist groups like Al Qaeda, or that America supported the bloody reign of the Khmer Rouge. There are endless examples of the evils which America has enacted in the world.

Democracy is a form of government which historically has worked very well for the American people, but the American colonists assumed this government voluntarily and of their own volition; it was not imposed upon them by a foreign power. (Arguably America is more of an oligarchy today than a real democratic republic, but that is a discussion for another book.) My point is that democracy forced upon another foreign country will never work; it worked for America because of cultural, philosophical, and spiritual values that the American colonial populace already held to be true, and the American revolutionaries were willing to assume responsibility for their own destiny, regardless of what the consequences of their actions might have been. The evidence of this mindset is built right into the language of the Declaration of Independence: "And for the support of this declaration, with a firm reliance on the protection of Divine Providence, we mutually pledge to each other our lives, our fortunes, and our sacred honor." But most other nations of the world are not ready for democracy; they lack a conviction concerning basic truths like the equality of all human beings. Therefore, America's efforts to "export democracy" to these peoples are misguided and have resulted in many other nations hating America and resenting her interference in their affairs.

Thus far I have only written about America's failings from a purely physical and philosophical perspective; much needs to be said about America from a spiritual and moral perspective also. We have, in prior chapters, discussed a great many of Mystery Babylon's moral failings in the eyes of God. We must remember that God has a different, completely objective view of the guilt and innocence of persons and nations: "Shall not the Judge of all the earth do right?" (Genesis 18:25) Like the ancient Neo-Babylonian Empire in Daniel 5, which we have examined already, America has been weighed in God's balances and "found wanting."

While we have discussed America's wickedness to a degree already, in the rest of this chapter we will examine some other aspects of America's sins before God which we have not already visited. We will look at these things from God's perspective, using God's own words from Scripture, so that there will be no mistake about America's condemnation.

(I would like to make a note here, before I am accused of being an American who hates his own country based upon these difficult things which I have written above. I am an extremely patriotic, loyal, law-abiding American citizen, from a family of patriotic Americans. My family's history is America's history; my ancestors were British, French, and German immigrants to this nation. Three of my grandparents served in various branches of the United States military; my father served; and I tried to join two different branches of the military on several separate occasions, but was ultimately disqualified from military service on a medical technicality. As a child, I greatly admired the great American patriot Nathan Hale, and I can quote his resounding last words by heart: "I only regret that I have but one life to lose for my country." But those who love America best are those who most grieve over her faults.)

God hates America's pride.

*"**These six things doth the LORD hate**: yea, seven are an **abomination unto him**:*

***A proud look**, a lying tongue, and hands that shed innocent blood,*

An heart that deviseth wicked imaginations, feet that be swift in running to mischief,

A false witness that speaketh lies, and he that soweth discord among brethren."

Proverbs 6:16-19

Pride is the very first thing on this list of evils which God reviles. Why does God hate human arrogance so much? Pride is the failure to understand that human status, achievement, and talent are conferred by God Himself; they are not qualities inherent to us which we can take credit for. Don't misunderstand these things; there is nothing wrong with having a sense of joy, satisfaction, or achievement for a job well done and worked hard for. But when we lift ourselves up and ignore that all our virtues, even the measure of faith which we have, are bestowed by God, we broken human beings invariably begin to think more highly of ourselves than we ought, putting ourselves above other people and even above God. This is the attitude of Mystery Babylon in Scripture:

*"And thou saidst, I shall be a lady for ever: **so that thou didst not lay these things to thy heart, neither didst remember the latter end of it**.*

*Therefore hear now this, thou that art given to pleasures, that dwellest carelessly, that sayest in thine heart, **I am, and none else beside me**; I shall not sit as*

a widow, neither shall I know the loss of children:"
Isaiah 47:7-8

Notice Babylon's self-satisfied declaration in Isaiah 47 verse 8: "I am, and none else beside me." Can you see the essential meaning of these words? Babylon says, "I am the only one who really matters, everyone else is beneath me." The entitled, superior attitude of modern America is disgusting in the eyes of the God of Heaven.

Can you see the beginnings of horrors in this attitude of arrogant pride? The Nazis believed in the superiority of the Aryan race; all others were subhuman, cattle to be used, abused, and discarded; the horrors of the Holocaust were born. The Russians believed that the motherland was superior to all the other nations; purges and pogroms and slaughter of ethnic groups ensued. The Japanese believed that their divine Emperor was blessed by the gods and that it was their destiny to rule the world; they had little mercy or consideration for defeated enemy prisoners of war. Ironically, none of these nations, which were allied with each other at the beginning of World War II, could ever have peacefully coexisted with each other later on; their separate beliefs in their own superiority would have ensured their eventual conflict and mutual destruction.

"Behold, I am against thee, O thou most proud, saith the Lord GOD of hosts: for thy day is come, the time that I will visit thee.

And the most proud shall stumble and fall, and none shall raise him up: and I will kindle a fire in his cities, and it shall devour all round about him."

Jeremiah 50:31-32

"How much she hath glorified herself, and lived deliciously, so much torment and sorrow give her: for she saith in her heart, I sit a queen, and am no widow, and shall see no sorrow."

Revelation 18:7

Jeremiah 51 has a sobering reminder for all those who would lift themselves up in pride; even as America lifts herself up, believing herself to be without peer, the God of Heaven, Who is *truly* without peer, swears by Himself that He will judge the proud Babylon:

"The LORD of hosts hath sworn by himself, saying, Surely I will fill thee with men, as with caterpillers; and they shall lift up a shout against thee.

He hath made the earth by his power, he hath established the world by his wisdom, and hath stretched out the heaven by his understanding.

When he uttereth his voice, there is a multitude of waters in the heavens; and he causeth the vapours to ascend from the ends of the earth: he maketh lightnings with rain, and bringeth forth the wind out of his treasures.

Every man is brutish by his knowledge; every founder is confounded by the graven image: for his molten image is falsehood, and there is no breath in them.

They are vanity, the work of errors: in the time of their visitation they shall perish."
Jeremiah 51:14-18

God hates America's sexual immorality.

Human sexuality is important to God for a number of reasons. God made marriage to be a good thing that brings joy, pleasure, comfort, and new life. It is not meant to be *only* fun, but also functional. We see also in Scriptures something that God calls a "great mystery" -- the truth that Biblical marriage is meant to reflect the relationship between God and His people:

"So ought men to love their wives as their own bodies. He that loveth his wife loveth himself.
For no man ever yet hated his own flesh; but nourisheth and cherisheth it, ***even as the Lord the church****:*
For we are members of his body, of his flesh, and of his bones.
For this cause shall a man leave his father and mother, and shall be joined unto his wife, and they two shall be one flesh.
This is a great mystery: but I speak concerning Christ and the church*."*
Ephesians 5:28-32

When human beings distort sexuality into something it was not meant to be; they are demonstrating their brokenness and wickedness before God. Sexual wickedness is an affront to God's intended order. I have seen no greater argument against the accidental origins of life taught by evolutionists than the existence of human gender, which was established by God:

"So God created man in his own image, in the image of God created he him; ***male and female created he them****."*

Genesis 1:27

"And he answered and said unto them, Have ye not read, that ***he which made them at the beginning made them male and female****,*

And said, For this cause shall a man leave father and mother, and shall cleave to his wife: and they twain shall be one flesh?"

Matthew 19:4-5

How could the genders have originated without a designer? In order for a species to propagate and thus survive, both genders must have arisen simultaneously and in a completed, functional form. American society is caught in the grasp of a relatively new movement reacting against physical gender; there are now any number of "genders" and people are "free" to choose whatever gender they wish to identify with. The homosexuality and other sexual deviances which America has embraced and celebrated are absolute folly and disgusting in God's estimation, demonstrating that those who practice them do not know God or His truth:

"Thou shalt not lie with mankind, as with womankind: it is abomination."
Leviticus 18:22

"And even as they did not like to retain God in their knowledge, God gave them over to ***a reprobate mind****, to do those things which are not convenient;*
Being filled with all ***unrighteousness, fornication, wickedness****, covetousness, maliciousness; full of envy, murder, debate, deceit, malignity; whisperers,*
Backbiters, haters of God, despiteful, proud, boasters, ***inventors of evil things****, disobedient to parents,*
Without understanding, ***covenantbreakers, without natural affection****, implacable, unmerciful:*
Who knowing the judgment of God, that they which commit such things are worthy of death, ***not only do the same, but have pleasure in them that do them****."*
Romans 1:28-32

God's perspective on human sexuality is clearly quite different from the views of modern American society. Sexual perversions, premarital sex, adultery, and divorce are all considered to be quite normal and even morally acceptable by modern standards. With the increasingly ubiquitous presence of pornographic and sexually explicit material in music and entertainment, even those who do not do such things themselves are increasingly tempted and invited to "take pleasure in those that do them."

If a strong, loving marriage is a picture of what the relationship between God and His people should look like, then the decline of marriage in America is symbolic of our nation's rejection of God and His righteousness. Pew Research Center has long traced the decline of marriage and the rise of divorce rates in the United States. According to the Annie E. Casey Foundation (AECF) and other sources, a little more than a third of all children in the United States are being raised in single-parent homes. AECF notes that these children are greatly disadvantaged compared to children raised with two parents; they are "more likely to drop out of school, to have or cause a teen pregnancy, and to experience a divorce in adulthood." Thus the downward trend of sexual immorality self-propagates.

God hates America's slaughter of innocent children.

We Americans like to believe that we are so progressive and enlighted, certainly more progressive and enlightened than, say, the backwards and superstitious pagans of ancient times, who worshipped idols and images made with hands and who sacrificed men, women, and children to appease some bloody deity. Ironically, Americans do all the same things that the ancient pagans once did; we have already discussed America's idolatry in a previous chapter. But America is also far bloodier than any pagan nation whose gods demanded human hearts or burnt offerings. At least those backwards pagans truly believed that their sacrifices to the gods could turn the fortunes of war, or bring down rains to end droughts, or cure a wasting plague. But here in America, we sacrifice our children upon the altars of selfishness and convenience.

I am referring, of course, to America's abortion of millions of unborn and partially born children. It is hard to calculate exactly how many abortions have been performed in the United States; the Centers for Disease Control (CDC) maintains statistics on abortion in the USA, but they rely on voluntary reporting by the states, and some states, like California, have not reported their abortion statistics to the CDC in two decades. The Guttmacher Institute also compiles abortion statistics from all fifty states by reaching out directly to abortion clinics, but they do not carry out their surveys every year. Between these two sources, it can be estimated that there have been over 60,000,000 abortions in the United States of America since 1973. No pagan civilization ever slaughtered more children than "enlightened" America.

A large portion of America's populace simply refuses to acknowledge the genocide that America has committed over the decades. We are told that women should "have a choice." Indeed they do, but choices have consequences. Even as America has weighed the lives of millions of infants, so God has weighed America in His balance of absolute justice and found her wanting.

God's judgment is already being felt by America for her national sin of abortion. The sixty million children who will never live are not here. They are not productive members of society, working and contributing their tax dollars into the system. They are not voting to steer the course of our nation. They are not consuming and thus supporting national agriculture and industry. They will not develop new, life-saving technologies or the cures for rare diseases. They will not be here to defend America from her enemies. To us, they are silent; we cannot hear their voices. But the God who told Cain, "Thy brother's blood cries unto Me from the ground!" remembers the innocent life that America has wantonly discarded. God knew each of those lost children when their elements had yet to be formed from the earth:

"My substance was not hid from thee, when I was made in secret, and curiously wrought in the lowest parts of the earth."

Psalm 139:15

Mark the words of the Lord Jesus Christ in the book of Luke, concerning those who offend (harm or abuse) little children:

"It were better for him that ***a millstone were hanged about his neck, and he cast into the sea****, than that he should offend one of these little ones."*
Luke 17:2

The God of Heaven, Whose Word tells us that children are a gift from Him, also gave us the following words concerning the fall of Mystery Babylon. Their connection with the dire words of our Lord in Luke 17:2 are chilling:

"And a mighty angel took up ***a stone like a great millstone, and cast it into the sea****, saying, Thus with violence shall that great city Babylon be thrown down, and shall be found no more at all."*
Revelation 18:21

America is bloodguilty before God because of her unbelief.

God clearly holds Mystery Babylon guilty of the blood of martyred prophets and saints:

"And I saw the woman ***drunken with the blood of the saints, and with the blood of the martyrs of Jesus****: and when I saw her, I wondered with great admiration."*
Revelation 17:6

"And after these things I heard a great voice of

much people in heaven, saying, Alleluia; Salvation, and glory, and honour, and power, unto the Lord our God:

For true and righteous are his judgments: for he hath judged the great whore, which did corrupt the earth with her fornication, and hath ***avenged the blood of his servants at her hand****.*

And again they said, Alleluia. And her smoke rose up for ever and ever."

Revelation 19:1-3

"And ***in her was found the blood of prophets, and of saints****, and of all that were slain upon the earth."*

Revelation 18:24

This is a curious condemnation, so I wanted to be certain to specifically address it in this book. You might say, "How can this be? America itself has historically been a Christian nation, and America has never targeted Jews or Christians!"

There is actually at least one historical example of the United States killing large populations of Christians. The Japanese city of Nagasaki had a very large Christian community (whose persecutions by the Japanese government had even at points involved torture and mass crucifixions) and the nuclear bomb that American forces dropped on that city detonated directly above Urakami Cathedral, the largest Christian church in eastern Asia at the time. (The church was chosen as a target from only a very few available visible landmarks in Nagasaki.) But the bombing of Nagasaki represents an anomaly in American history, and was clearly not the intentional targeting of God's saints. It is clear that God's assessment of America's bloodguiltiness must derive from some other of her sins.

I will mention that I need to be careful concerning Revelation 18:24. Does this verse mean that Mystery Babylon is *guilty* of the blood of prophets, saints, and all nations of the earth, or does this verse mean that these are some of the people who will perish with Mystery Babylon when she falls? Both of these truths are clearly supported elsewhere by verses we have already seen, and while I am not sure specifically which of these meanings is meant, you may clearly see from the other verses above (and others which I did not put here) that the God of Heaven considers Babylon to be guilty of the blood of His people.

Why is America guilty of the blood of prophets and saints? Consider a similar passage from the New Testament:

"Truly ye bear witness that ye allow the deeds of your fathers: for they indeed killed them, and ye build their sepulchres.

Therefore also said the wisdom of God, I will send them prophets and apostles, and some of them they shall slay and persecute:

That the blood of all the prophets, which was shed

from the foundation of the world, ***may be required of this generation****;*

From the blood of Abel unto the blood of Zacharias, which perished between the altar and the temple: ***verily I say unto you, It shall be required of this generation****."*

Luke 11:48-51

Do you follow what our Lord Jesus Christ is saying in this passage of Scripture? God sent prophets and apostles to His people to preach repentence of sins and God's righteousness, but the Jews hated and killed those messengers because they loved their wickedness. They would not believe God's words. In Luke 11 above, Jesus tells the Jews of His own time that even though they did not themselves kill God's prophets and apostles (their ancestors did), because they assented to the same wickednesses of their forebears and rejected Jesus Christ's truth, they will also be held guilty of the blood of the prophets and apostles. Those who have been given more truth and warning from God are held more accountable for their unbelief in God's eyes.

Mystery Babylon, America, is guilty of the blood of God's prophets and of the blood of the martyred saints of the Lord Jesus Christ because America has chosen to reject God and His truth. America assents to and perpetrates all the ancient wickedness of all the pagan civilizations which came before her and which hated, persecuted, and even killed God's people.

Mystery Babylon, America, while an actual modern nation, is also a *figure*, a spiritual *symbol* representing the pinnacle of godless humanity's pride, wickedness, and achievement. When the saints depicted in Revelation 19 shall see her destruction, they shall assent with God that His judgment was righteous, and that the blood of all the saints will have been avenged for all of Babylon's sins!

God has been merciful to Mystery Babylon (America).

You may be wondering at this point, "If America is so wicked in God's eyes, why has she been so prosperous? Why hasn't God judged her long before this?" Indeed, America's time for judgment is long overdue (in the sense that America is more than deserving of it), and despite her wickedness, America is the most prosperous and comfortable nation which has ever existed. The answer to these question lies in the nature of God Himself.

Our Lord Jesus Christ said these words:

"Ye have heard that it hath been said, Thou shalt love thy neighbour, and hate thine enemy.

But I say unto you, ***Love your enemies, bless them that curse you, do good to them that hate you, and pray for them which despitefully use you, and persecute you****;*

That ye may be the children of your Father which is in heaven: for ***he maketh his sun to rise on the evil and on the good, and sendeth rain on the just and on the unjust*.***"*

Matthew 5:43-45

These were not merely idle words on the part of Jesus Christ; we read in the Bible that God's purpose in sending Jesus to earth was that Jesus Christ should die for the sins of all humankind, whose wickedness is an affront to God. God showers good things down upon humanity, even giving good things to those who do not deserve them. God tells us to love our enemies, because God Himself extends His love to *His* enemies: wicked, fallen, rebellious humanity. How very much like God to bless wicked Babylon even when America opposes Him! The God of Heaven has given America more than any other nation has been given:

- America has been given wealth and comforts above all the other nations of history and the modern era.
- America has been given power and victory over all the nations of the earth.
- America has been given great security and rule of law, in contrast to many lawless, dangerous regions of the world.
- America has been given a Christian witness and warning through the Bible, through thousands of true Christian churches, through a Christian

heritage, and through millions of Christians living within the United States today.

- God has given a specific sign which will precede America's judgment in Jeremiah 51:46; few nations have been blessed with such a specific warning of future destruction.

No other nation of men has been blessed like Mystery Babylon. God has shown more longsuffering patience towards her than any other nation. God has given Mystery Babylon every chance to repent and more warnings than He ever gave any other wicked kingdom. But the time of merciful forbearance is coming to an end; God has sworn that He will judge Mystery Babylon:

"For thus saith the LORD of hosts, the God of Israel; The daughter of Babylon is like a threshingfloor, it is time to thresh her: yet a little while, and the time of her harvest shall come."
Jeremiah 51:33

Chapter 7:
America's Coming Destruction

Isaiah 47, Jeremiah 50 and 51, Revelation 16:19-19:3

~

"Behold, the nations are as a drop of a bucket, and are counted as the small dust of the balance: behold, he taketh up the isles as a very little thing.

All nations before him are as nothing; and they are counted to him less than nothing, and vanity."

Isaiah 40:15, 17

How will America be destroyed?

I need to begin this chapter with a disclaimer. There are many things in God's Word which are clear, plain, and certain. We can see that many aspects of Scripture's predictions of Mystery Babylon's destruction are very straightforward. Other details are hidden and will not be certain until they come to pass. In this chapter, we will discuss the coming destruction of the United States of America and how it *might* take place. That this destruction *will* take place is certain;

God has sworn by Himself that He will judge Mystery Babylon. The exact form of that judgment, while described in astonishing detail in the chapters of Scripture which we have been examining, is unclear because of our human inability to see exactly what will happen even in the near future.

So as we progress through this chapter, I wish to make it plain now that I will describe what I see in the Scriptures, but my particular interpretation of the progression of events may be very flawed. God does make certain signs explicitly clear, however, and since these are certain I will emphasize them greatly when we reach that point.

The trouble seems to begin in the Middle East, as usual.

Scattered throughout the chapters concerning Mystery Babylon's fall are statements by God that Mystery Babylon is responsible for undermining Israel and causing her harm:

"Israel is a scattered sheep; the lions have driven him away: first the king of Assyria hath devoured him; and last this Nebuchadrezzar king of Babylon hath broken his bones.

Therefore thus saith the LORD of hosts, the God of Israel; Behold, I will punish the king of Babylon and his land, as I have punished the king of Assyria.

And I will bring Israel again to his habitation, and

he shall feed on Carmel and Bashan, and his soul shall be satisfied upon mount Ephraim and Gilead."
Jeremiah 50:17-19

The duality of Biblical prophecy can be very confusing as we try to understand it. The Encyclopedia Britannica mentions that this name "Nebuchadrezzar" (notice the letter difference) can be used interchangeably with the name Nebuchadnezzar, whom we have already met in Daniel 2. There are elements of Jeremiah 50:17-19 which could be applied to Nebuchadnezzar and his conquest of Jerusalem, but there are elements which do not apply and which I believe reference the Mystery Babylon that Jeremiah chapter 50 is so clearly speaking about. For example, Babylon under Nebuchadnezzar was *not* punished for their treatment of Israel.

In relation to Mystery Babylon, these verses in Jeremiah 50 seem to describe a future scenario between Israel, Iran, and America. One reason for this is that Mount Bashan, referenced in verse 19, is currently in territory possessed by the Kingdom of Jordan. Boundaries and locations in the region can be very confusing (and are hardly my forte), so I will here give a little bit of background to help you understand some of the basics. Large portions of southern Syria are lawless and ungoverned due to the ongoing Syrian civil war. Large portions of Jordan are also lawless and ungoverned, and Israel has considered stepping in and policing those regions in order to maintain her own security, but has not done so because Israel knows that such action would be perceived as unwarranted aggression by the international community. Taking advantage of the tremendous power vacuum in this area around the north of Israel, Iran (which is perhaps the Assyria in Jeremiah 50) has made a concerted effort to establish supply lines through southern Syria over into Lebanon, so that the Iranian government can funnel weapons and supplies to the extremist group Hezbollah, a sworn enemy of the state of Israel, which Iran is training and funding. (Interrestingly, the United States indirectly assists Hezbollah also, by supplying and training Lebanon's military.) Israel has been launching drone strikes (and likely intervening in other ways also) against Iranian convoys in southern Syria in order to prevent the establishment of this Iran-Lebanon supply chain. The region is tremendously unstable and also a bit of a powder keg between Israel and Iran, which could ignite at any moment.

I suspect that Jeremiah 50:17-19 hints at another future conflict between Israel and Iran. It is unclear what America's involvement in this conflict will be, but clearly it will be detrimental to Israel and will represent a betrayal of the historic alliance between Israel and America. Perhaps Iran will establish a presence in southern Syria and Israel will decide to intervene with actual troops on the ground, a politically dangerous move for Israel. Given the current tensions between the United States and Iran

(America has accused Iran of attacking oil tankers; Iran shot down an American surveillance drone; President Trump strongly considered air strikes as retribution) it is likely that the United States would commit to assisting Israel in such a situation. But perhaps at a critical moment, after pledging military support to Israel, America suddenly will back out of its commitment, perhaps due to a change in government after a major election. Israel will be left in an exposed position alone, and will suffer and take casualties for the betrayal.

Or perhaps the "breaking of Israel's bones" portrayed in Jeremiah will be something less dramatic. Great leaps of progress have been made in the relationship between America and Israel under President Trump, including the relocation of the United States embassy in Israel to Jerusalem. Will a new President or Congress revert all the positive changes between America and Jerusalem, making America undermine Israel instead of supporting her? God promised in His Word to bless those nations which bless Israel, and to curse those nations which curse Israel. While America is a wicked nation worthy of God's judgment, God will keep His Word while America honors Israel. The fall of Mystery Babylon will likely begin with some betrayal of Israel by the United States.

America will be engulfed in another great civil war.

Jeremiah 50 seems to portray a regime change in America which leads to her betrayal of her ally Israel, initiating God's judgment on America. A regime change also explains something that we see very clearly in Jeremiah 51: **America will face another devastating civil war at some point in the future.** The Scriptures are absolutely clear about this, and **the advent of the next civil war is God's sign to His people that judgment is coming soon; get out of Babylon!** Consider very carefully the message of Jeremiah 51 verses 45 to 47:

"My people, go ye out of the midst of her, and deliver ye every man his soul from the fierce anger of the LORD.

And lest your heart faint, and ye fear for the rumour that shall be heard in the land; a rumour shall both come one year, and after that in another year shall come a rumour, and ***violence in the land, ruler against ruler****.*

Therefore, behold, the days come, that I will do judgment upon the graven images of Babylon*: and her whole land shall be confounded, and all her slain shall fall in the midst of her."*

Jeremiah 51:45-47

This is God's warning to His people living in the United States of America, and it could not be more clear. There will be rumors in the land about the civil conflict which is coming, years of rumors. Do not be afraid because of the rumors! The true sign that America's judgment is at hand will be the beginning of the civil war: "**violence in the land, ruler against ruler**." Take notice of this warning, and keep an eye on current events. These things are coming; God has promised it!

Rumors of civil war are already here. I will dedicate an entire chapter later on to exploring how a new American civil war might arise, because this is a very important sign from God Himself. I will briefly mention here that major newspaper articles have explored the possibility of another American civil war already. A recent survey of voting adults in America showed that over 25% believe that the United States will be involved in another civil war *within five years*. If you are familiar with American politics, it is not hard to see how the outcome of a Presidential election could result in civil unrest if the results of the election are conclusively shown to have been manipulated by one side or the other. Some patriotic Americans, myself included, would consider America to be dead if our Constitution were ever to be undermined, especially the Second Amendment. An attempt to confiscate citizens' firearms would be seen as a tyrannical act reminiscent of the British attempt to capture the American colonists' weapons at Lexington and Concord in order to ensure their peaceful compliance with the British crown.

God's Word is very clear that there will be conflict within the land of Mystery Babylon even before the northern alliance rains destruction upon her:

"A sound of battle is in the land, and of great destruction."
Jeremiah 50:22

"The LORD of hosts hath sworn by himself, saying, Surely I will fill thee with men, as with caterpillers; and they shall lift up a shout against thee."
Jeremiah 51:14

An alliance of great nations from the north will launch a decisive, crippling attack upon the United States of America.

America will be completely distracted and in disarray because of the civil war raging chaotically within her borders. That opportunity will be far too great to pass up for America's historic rivals and adversaries; an "assembly of great nations":

"For, lo, I will raise and cause to come up against Babylon an assembly of great nations from the north country: and they shall set themselves in array against her; from thence she shall be taken: their arrows shall be as of a mighty expert man; none shall return in vain."
Jeremiah 50:9

"Behold, a people shall come from the north, and a

great nation, and many kings shall be raised up from the coasts of the earth.

They shall hold the bow and the lance: they are cruel, and will not shew mercy: their voice shall roar like the sea, and they shall ride upon horses, every one put in array, like a man to the battle, against thee, O daughter of Babylon.

The king of Babylon hath heard the report of them, and his hands waxed feeble: anguish took hold of him, and pangs as of a woman in travail."

Jeremiah 50:41-43

It is unclear exactly how large this coalition will be, but Revelation mentions the ten horns of the terrible beast which hate the Whore of Babylon and devour her:

"And the ten horns which thou sawest upon the beast, these shall hate the whore, and shall make her desolate and naked, and shall eat her flesh, and burn her with fire."

Revelation 17:16

As we have already seen, the book of Revelation is clear that these nations which overthrow America will one day form the core of the Antichrist's one-world government, a true evil New World Order. Can we ascertain anything about the identity of these great nations? Yes, we can; Jeremiah gives us some very telling clues:

"Set ye up a standard in the land, blow the trumpet among the nations, prepare the nations against her, call together against her the ***kingdoms of Ararat, Minni, and Ashchenaz****; appoint a captain against her; cause the horses to come up as the rough caterpillers.*

Prepare against her ***the nations with the kings of the Medes, the captains thereof, and all the rulers thereof, and all the land of his dominion****."*

Jeremiah 51:27-28

The identities of some of these nations are quite clear. The "north" and the "king of the north" in Scripture is largely accepted by many Biblical scholars to be a reference to Soviet Russia, that great and powerful nation north of Israel. (Again, I recommend reading some of Joel Rosenberg's excellent non-fiction books if you are interested in the subject of end times prophecy.) The "kingdom of Ararat" is plain enough: Turkey. "Minni" is a region of northwestern Iran in the vicinity of the East and West Azerbaijan Provinces of Iran, near several small nations between Iran and Turkey. I suspect that Jeremiah's reference to the "kingdom of Minni" is not actually a reference to Iran itself though; because Jeremiah's later reference to the "kings of the Medes" can very well encompass the nation of Iran. Perhaps Minni is the Muslin nation of Azerbaijan just north of Iran's Azerbaijan provinces. Jeremiah's reference to the "kingdom of Ashchenaz" is also fairly plain; this is a reference to the Scythian (barbarian) territories of ancient times, which are the Slavic nations of today. This region could well encompass vast swaths of north and eastern Europe and northern Asia. Russia is likely meant by this term, but perhaps also some of the Soviet satellite nations as well. If Ashchenaz here is being used to reference the ancient Scythian territories, nations like Kazakhstan, Uzbekistan, and Turkmenistan could well be included. It is noteworthy that Kazakhstan, Uzbekistan, and Turkmenistan are all former Soviet republics and are predominantly Muslim nations, being 70%, 88%, and 93% Muslim respectively.

Does a great coalition of Russia, Iran, Turkey, and their satellite states make sense in light of the current geopolitical situation? Very much so. Russia, generally historically ambivalent towards religion, has become increasingly friendly to Islam and to Muslim refugees over the past decades, and Iran has long been a proxy of Russia in the Middle East. Biblical scholars have been increasingly leaning towards the idea that the Antichrist's future kingdom may be a Muslim alliance of nations. Turkey's inclusion in this list is not surprising either; Turkey and Russia have been strenthening their ties and collaborating concerning their actions in Syria. Turkey, though a NATO nation and "ally" of the United States, has increasingly gravitated towards Russia as the relationship between the western and eastern power blocs has grown more polarized. Turkey has been forced to choose a side, and it is choosing Russia. For example, when Russia and Turkey settled upon an arrangement for Turkey to purchase Russia's cutting edge S-400 missile defense system, America protested and informed Turkey that if they went ahead with the Russian missile deal, a previous deal with the United States for Turkey to purchase American-made F-35 fighter planes would be canceled. Turkey made it clear that they resented the United States' ultimatum and they purchased the Russian missiles.

The Scriptures make it clear (and we will discuss both of these) that there will be both conventional warfare employed against Mystery Babylon's holdings by this coalition of great nations, as well as something that humanity has long feared: a massive nuclear first strike.

Nuclear devastation will rain down upon the United States of America.

How will this coalition of powerful nations, led by Russia, destroy the United States of America? Over and over again, the chapters of the Bible which detail the destruction of Mystery Babylon mention *arrows* and *fire*. Let me count these references: six references to arrows and eight references to fire in Jeremiah and Revelation. Consider some of the verses which discuss arrows:

"For, lo, I will raise and cause to come up against Babylon an assembly of great nations from the north

country: and they shall set themselves in array against her; from thence she shall be taken: ***their arrows shall be as of a mighty expert man; none shall return in vain****."*

Jeremiah 50:9

"Put yourselves in array against Babylon round about: ***all ye that bend the bow, shoot at her, spare no arrows****: for she hath sinned against the LORD."*

Jeremiah 50:14

*"****Call together the archers against Babylon: all ye that bend the bow****, camp against it round about; let none thereof escape:* ***recompense her according to her work; according to all that she hath done, do unto her****: for she hath been proud against the LORD, against the Holy One of Israel."*

Jeremiah 50:29

In the ancient world, arrows were a secondary weapon of war; decisive victory was generally determined by infantry or cavalry. Most ancient militaries utilized some kind of marksmen however, whether archers, skirmishers, or slingers, to soften up armies of heavier troops for eventual close-up melee combat. The arrows depicted in the Biblical fall of Mystery Babylon are portrayed as much more potent; they are a decisive and devastating weapon which will not miss. Based on their capabilities and their results, these are clearly nuclear weapons. I think it is interesting that Jeremiah 50:29 says that Mystery Babylon's attackers will do to her what she has done to others; America today is the only nation which has ever used nuclear weapons against another nation during wartime.

The results of these "arrows" are widespread desolation, plague (radiation), and fire which will render the land inhospitable for human life. We will see these things in more detail in a moment. The question must be asked at this point, "Why would America's military defenses not come to her aid during a nuclear bombardment by a foreign power?" Considering America's military defense capabilities, this is an excellent question that deserves a thorough answer.

There are several reasons why America's technology (the Bible refers to it as "sorceries") will not save her. The first is that the devastating future American civil war will be all-encompassing for America's soldiers; indeed, America may not have a unified military any longer at this point, with the National Guard units of various states fighting each other and with America's regular military defecting to protect their families or joining state forces in the civil conflict. The second reason is that America's missile defenses and other technology will have been compromised from within by enemy sleeper agents, spies, hackers, and saboteurs. I am not speaking hypothetically; Russia, China, and North Korea among others have long seen the value of using hackers to disrupt and manipulate conditions. I can think of several relevant headlines pertaining to hackers striking American infrastructure in recent years: a factory had safety protocols disabled remotely by hackers, resulting in a massive fire, a prison's doors were all remotely unlocked in the middle of the night, causing chaos. (Some years ago, my father noticed and kept track of a string of industrial accidents which seemed to have been caused by remote interference; he took steps to make authorities aware of the potential threat.) In our increasingly computer-connected world, those connections become security hazards and exploits for America's enemies. Enemy software technologies are already attempting to compromise America's ability to defend herself from a massive missile strike. The third reason is that many of America's rivals are now focusing on technologies that specifically counter those technologies upon which America's military and defenses rely: American communications and intelligence. Russia and China, specifically, have realized the need to counter American technology and have focused their research on two technologies which give them an advantage against America in a conflict: faster, longer range missiles for delivering warheads and electromagnetic pulse (EMP) weapon technology. EMPs have the ability to disrupt electronics and communications over a vast area; a nuclear weapon detonated high above a region, for example, can generate an electromagnetic pulse which could cripple vehicles, cell phones, satellites, and even unprotected portions of the power grid. While America's enemies constantly attempt to find chinks in her armor, a recent Pentagon paper made the uncomfortable assessment that America's military has become less vigilant and adaptable; we have become accustomed to our military dominance and have become complacent.

America's hope of survival will be gone before she even realizes what is happening. The northern coalition's bombardment will likely begin in the west; America's bases and countermeasures in the Pacific, Hawaii, and Alaska will be neutralized and the West Coast of the United States will be hit hard:

"One post shall run to meet another, and one messenger to meet another, to shew the king of Babylon that his city is taken at one end,

And that the passages are stopped, and the reeds they have burned with fire, and the men of war are affrighted."

Jeremiah 51:31-32

The devastation will be so sudden and so crippling that America will be unable to counter or retaliate; how would America even possibly retaliate against ten nations launching nuclear strikes against her at once? With power and communications being down across vast swaths of American territory, and smoke choking the atmosphere over the entire continent, US military command could be unable to even reach out to America's nuclear fleet for a counterattack.

America's technology, in which she trusts for her security, will fail her utterly, and darkness will overtake the nation. American leadership and advisors will be in chaos and confusion, unable to act decisively:

"Stand now with thine enchantments, and with the multitude of thy sorceries, wherein thou hast laboured from thy youth; if so be thou shalt be able to profit, if so be thou mayest prevail.

Thou art wearied in the multitude of thy counsels. Let now the astrologers, the stargazers, the monthly prognosticators, stand up, and save thee from these things that shall come upon thee.

Behold, they shall be as stubble; the fire shall burn them; they shall not deliver themselves from the power of the flame: there shall not be a coal to warm at, nor fire to sit before it."

Isaiah 47:12-14

Raging firestorms result from the bombings, and conditions exacerbate the spreading fires.

The Scriptures are clear that Mystery Babylon will cease to be a world power in just a single day (Revelation 18:8, 10), but after the wave of nuclear strikes it will take some time for raging fires to consume the American homeland. While most of the wise who foresaw the destruction have long since left

America at this point, some refugees who were not incinerated in the initial attack may survive and be able to flee. The Bible suggests that America will already have been in a drought because of God's judgment; the nation will be like dry tinder to the cataclysmic holocaust:

*Therefore thus saith the LORD; Behold, I will plead thy cause, and take vengeance for thee; and **I will dry up her sea, and make her springs dry**."*
Jeremiah 51:36

*"**A drought is upon her waters; and they shall be dried up**: for it is the land of graven images, and they are mad upon their idols."*
Jeremiah 50:38

The first verses of Jeremiah 51 seem to describe a phenomenon known as a firestorm:

"Thus saith the LORD; Behold, I will raise up against Babylon, and against them that dwell in the midst of them that rise up against me, a destroying wind;
And will send unto Babylon fanners, that shall fan her, and shall empty her land: for in the day of trouble they shall be against her round about."
Jeremiah 51:1-2

Humanity has seen devastating firestorms in the past. A firestorm is a large fire so intense that it creates its own updraft, which pulls air towards the inferno from all directions around it. One might think that this would keep the fire from spreading outward, but this wind has the opposite effect; it agitates the leading edge of the mass of flames and causes the blaze to spread even more quickly. The heat generated by a firestorm is tremendous, and these blazes can spontaneously ignite combustible materials hundreds of feet away, or even project such heat onto a distant opposing slope that the treeline there spontaneously combusts as well. A jetstream in the vicinity of a firestorm can exacerbate the phenomenon and greatly magnify the devastation.

Firestorms can arise naturally as a result of wildfires, or can arise in the aftermath of an intense bombing. They were part of the aftereffects of the nuclear bombings of Hiroshima and Nagasaki, for example. A possible side effect to a firestorm can be the appearance of a tornado of flame, called a "fire whirl." After the Allied bombings of the German city of Dresden during World War II, a tornado of fire appeared which was so intensely hot that it incinerated a crowd of 15,000 people in less than twenty minutes.

Americans are familiar with the experience of wildfires; I have been privileged to be able to travel to Montana several times in the last few years and have seen several wildfires for myself. Even a small wildfire, though an ordinary occurrence in that region, requires great efforts by firefighting crews to control it. But the fires which will sweep America after her bombing will be unlike any other. America will burn for months, or possibly even years, and eventually those brave souls who attempt to extinguish the inferno will give up in despair and flee:

"Thus saith the LORD of hosts; The broad walls of Babylon shall be utterly broken, and her high gates shall be burned with fire; and ***the people shall labour in vain, and the folk in the fire, and they shall be weary****."*
Jeremiah 51:58

"We would have healed Babylon, but she is not healed: forsake her, and let us go every one into his own country: for ***her judgment reacheth unto heaven, and is lifted up even to the skies****."*
Jeremiah 51:9

As we have seen already in previous chapters, all those who do commerce with America by sea will sit afar off, astonished at the smoke of her destruction and afraid to approach for fear of the radiation, extreme heat, fire, smoke, and rioting crowds of desperate refugees:

"Therefore shall her plagues come in one day, death, and mourning, and famine; and she shall be utterly burned with fire: for strong is the Lord God who judgeth her.

And the kings of the earth, who have committed

fornication and lived deliciously with her, shall bewail her, and lament for her, when they shall see the smoke of her burning,

Standing afar off for the fear of her torment, saying, Alas, alas, that great city Babylon, that mighty city! for in one hour is thy judgment come."

Revelation 18:8-10

The nuclear strikes may trigger other cataclysmic events as well; there are hints in Jeremiah and Revelation that flooding and earthquakes will be a part of Mystery Babylon's judgment. Much has been made in recent decades of the looming dangers of some of California's fault lines, or the Yellowstone supervolcano in the middle of the continent. Will a nuclear attack trigger other seismic events which will release even more devastation, collapsing and flooding large portions of the United States of America? It is impossible to say with the limited knowledge we have at hand for the time being; the future will tell.

New York City's bridges will be blocked and her remaining saltwater marshes will burn.

"And that the passages are stopped, and the reeds they have burned with fire, and the men of war are affrighted."

Jeremiah 51:32

The Hebrew word which is rendered in this

verse as "passages" is rendered elsewhere in the King James version of the Bible as a "ford," or river crossing. In modern America the majority of our river crossings are made via bridges, instead of fording the waters directly. This verse suggests a blockage of America's bridges, perhaps due to choking traffic fleeing from the fiery destruction. The area around Manhattan Island used to be predominantly a saltwater marsh, but over time as the city has grown these marshes have shrunk significantly. As of this present time, however, there are still approximately 200 acres of saltwater marshes around the northern tip of Manhattan. Will this area be covered by a burning oil slick? Will it catch fire some other way? About ten years ago, a researcher discovered completely by accident that salt water will release hydrogen and burn violently when exposed to certain specific radio frequencies. Perhaps widespread radiation on an unprecedented scale will actually ignite large areas of coastal salt water.

America will be utterly desolate, inhabited only by wild animals.

The Bible describes in great detail the coming desolation of America. It will become a fire-scorched, barren wasteland, its destruction rivaling that of the ancient wicked cities of Sodom and Gomorrah. It will be uninhabited forever, except by wild desert animals and mournful birds:

"Therefore shall evil come upon thee; thou shalt not know from whence it riseth: and mischief shall fall upon thee; thou shalt not be able to put it off: and desolation shall come upon thee suddenly, which thou shalt not know."

Isaiah 47:11

"For out of the north there cometh up a nation against her, ***which shall make her land desolate, and none shall dwell therein: they shall remove, they shall depart, both man and beast****."*

Jeremiah 50:3

"Your mother shall be sore confounded; she that bare you shall be ashamed: behold, ***the hindermost of the nations shall be a wilderness, a dry land, and a desert****.*

Because of the wrath of the LORD ***it shall not be inhabited, but it shall be wholly desolate****: every one that goeth by Babylon shall be astonished, and hiss at all her plagues."*

Jeremiah 50:12-13

"Come against her from the utmost border, open her storehouses: ***cast her up as heaps, and destroy her utterly: let nothing of her be left****."*

Jeremiah 50:26

"Therefore ***the wild beasts of the desert with the wild beasts of the islands shall dwell there****,*

and the owls shall dwell therein: and ***it shall be no more inhabited for ever; neither shall it be dwelt in from generation to generation****.*

As God overthrew Sodom and Gomorrah and the neighbour cities thereof, saith the LORD; so ***shall no man abide there, neither shall any son of man dwell therein****."*

Jeremiah 50:39-40

"And they shall not take of thee a stone for a corner, nor a stone for foundations; but ***thou shalt be desolate for ever****, saith the LORD."*

Jeremiah 51:26

"And the land shall tremble and sorrow: for every purpose of the LORD shall be performed against Babylon, ***to make the land of Babylon a desolation without an inhabitant****."*

Jeremiah 51:29

"And ***Babylon shall become heaps, a dwellingplace for dragons****, an astonishment, and an hissing,* ***without an inhabitant****."*

Jeremiah 51:37

*"****Her cities are a desolation, a dry land, and a wilderness, a land wherein no man dwelleth****, neither doth any son of man pass thereby."*

Jeremiah 51:43

"Then shalt thou say, O LORD, thou hast spoken against this place, to cut it off, that ***none shall remain in it, neither man nor beast, but that it shall be desolate for ever****."*

Jeremiah 51:62

"And he cried mightily with a strong voice, saying, Babylon the great is fallen, is fallen, and is ***become the habitation of devils, and the hold of every foul spirit, and a cage of every unclean and hateful bird****."*

Revelation 18:2

If it isn't already clear from the description of Mystery Babylon's desolation, this is not ancient Babylon we are discussing. We know that bricks from ancient Babylon were scavenged for centuries by local peoples for their building projects. God makes it clear in Jeremiah 51:26 that no one will be reusing America's rubble to rebuild anything.

Perhaps you have never heard of a man named Ron Wyatt. Wyatt was a very humble, down-to-earth Christian and amateur archaeologist. With God's direction, he was able to locate a great many sites of Biblical significance, including the site of Mount Sinai (not in the Sinai Peninsula!) and the Red Sea Crossing of the book of Exodus (not the western arm of the Red Sea!). By studying the Scriptures, he was able to ascertain the locations of the five Biblical "cities of the plain" which were judged by God for their wickedness, including the well known cities of Sodom and Gomorrah. Ron Wyatt visited one of these sites and took video and samples of sulphur spheres of a purity which is not found elsewhere in nature. The remains of the city walls and local terrain had been reduced by God's rain of fire and brimstone into a chalky, crumbling white ash. It was a completely barren and inhospitable landscape. Such will be America's coming utter destruction.

The word translated as "dragons" in Jeremiah 51:37 is perhaps better rendered today as "scavengers." We see that the wasted Mystery Babylon will be home to vultures and other "unclean and hateful birds," and perhaps some small rodents or other desert life used to eking out an existence where there is no water and scant food. No human or domesticated animal will inhabit America again, and her state will be a constant reminder of God's judgment for those who see it. It is likely that vast swaths of Canada and Mexico will also be caught up in America's conflagration.

Many American refugees who flee abroad will have a difficult new life trying to make a living in foreign lands.

"Come down, and sit in the dust, O virgin daughter of Babylon, sit on the ground: ***there is no throne****, O daughter of the Chaldeans: for* ***thou shalt no more be called tender and delicate****.*

Take the millstones, and grind meal:

uncover thy locks, make bare the leg, uncover the thigh, pass over the rivers.*"*

Isaiah 47:1-2

America's refugees will pass into other lands, where their standard of living will be much different from that to which they are accustomed. Some of the more misfortunate will end up in nations which will also be conquered by the northern coalition of powers which destroyed America.

America's outlying territories and protectorates will be swallowed up by her conquerors.

"And Chaldea shall be a spoil: all that spoil her shall be satisfied, saith the LORD."

Jeremiah 50:10

There are several references to the plundering of Mystery Babylon by her conquerors. I suspect that this means the American homeland will be utterly destroyed, but outlying territories and possessions, including military bases and perhaps even financial assets and companies, will be seized by the coalition of nations who have just destroyed the United States. Such is America's vast wealth, that even while the majority of her riches have been vaporized, there is still enough to satisfy all the nations that conspired to wipe America out.

The Russian bear-kingdom of Daniel 7 will become the dominant world superpower.

"And behold another beast, a second, like to a bear, and it raised up itself on one side, and it had three ribs in the mouth of it between the teeth of it: and they said thus unto it, Arise, devour much flesh."
Daniel 7:5

Russia, the bear beast of Daniel 7 will replace America, which is the winged lion, Mystery Babylon, and spiritual successor to ancient Babylon. This will be a dark time for humanity, for the chief characteristic of the bear-kingdom, as we have seen, is its destructive devouring of flesh. This new power will likely be much more hostile towards Christianity and Israel than its preceding superpower, and this Russian-led axis of nations will be driven to conquer and dominate.

What do the three ribs in the bear's mouth represent? It is uncertain, but I personally suspect that these represent some of the world's large democratic nations, perhaps nations of Anglo origins like Australia, New Zealand, Canada, or Great Britain. Those first three are the most likely candidates; Canada will be greatly weakened by the vast devastation along its southern border and the tremendous influx of refugees. Without the United States as her shield, she would easily fall to invasion and might even capitulate entirely without a fight.

Likewise Australia would have no chance against the northern coalition depicted in the Scriptures. Other American allies like Japan or Taiwan will be in very precarious positions with the disappearance of American dominance.

The nuclear strikes against America will have lasting geopolitical and environmental consequences.

The simultaneous release of energy represented in a coordinated nuclear strike capable of destroying a nation of the size of America will be staggering, perhaps even incalculable, and it will have a shocking effect upon global weather, climate, agriculture, and wildlife. There are other plagues in other Bible passages associated with the end times and perhaps some of these will have their roots in the nuclear holocaust which will extinguish America. There are plagues describing widespread drought and famine, the death of large percentages of life in the oceans, and of new and wasting diseases. As resources become scarce, wars and conflict over those resources will intensify. Many, many people will perish as history nears its final, bloody climax.

The Bible describes the smoke of America's burning several times over, and this choking fume will likely dilute the sunlight reaching Earth's surface for years or even decades. The temperature changes and changes to vegetation and crops that this will bring will result in more erosion and sea level rise. Species will become extinct at an increasingly rapid rate. The avarice and power-lust of wicked men will make life on Earth seem more and more like Hell.

The extinction of the American bison?

"Slay all her bullocks; let them go down to the slaughter: woe unto them! for their day is come, the time of their visitation."
Jeremiah 50:27

There were a great many minor points that I could not fully explore simply for the sake of brevity, but I will share this one. I cannot be dogmatic about this particular point, but it is one of the first things that came to mind when I read this verse in Jeremiah. The American bison (known colloquially as a "buffalo," though it technically is not) is a national icon, and great efforts have been made to stabilize the species and keep it from extinction. While the buffalo population is no longer anywhere near what it once was at its peak, the population is now stable at about half a million animals. Sadly, it seems that when America falls, this American symbol may die with her.

The smoke of America's burning will ascend "for ever and ever."

"And again they said, Alleluia. And her smoke rose

up for ever and ever."
Revelation 19:3

The implications of this verse are staggering to contemplate; what does it mean? There are at least two possibilities to consider. The first is that this verse is to be taken absolutely literally; the smoke of Mystery Babylon's destruction will literally ascend for the remainder of human history. This is not so outrageous a possibility as one might think; the aftermath of the 9/11 terrorist attacks on the World Trade Center demonstrated that fires can burn for weeks or even months on end. There is are even examples of fires burning for decades; the Centralia mine fire, which began when a coal seam ignited in a mine in Pennsylvania, has been burning for over 50 years. The fire is largely underground, but the coal mine shafts and tunnels funnel air and vent smoke to keep the blaze perpetually burning. It is too dangerous, expensive, and technically difficult to be able to put out the mine fires, so they have been left alone to run their course.

Another explanation for this verse is simply that in a spiritual sense, Mystery Babylon is an illustration of the absolute and inescapable nature of God's judgment of wickedness. His judgment, when it falls, will be *final* and *permanent*. Because of this, the destruction of America will serve as an eternal memorial to all future generations that God's judgment of evil is inevitable. Either of these explanations, the literal or the spiritual, are quite adequate, and I personally feel that both are likely to be meant by Revelation 19:3.

God's Purposes in Judging Mystery Babylon (America)

We see in the Scriptures that the God of Heaven is an intentional Being; He does not move or act without purpose. The Scriptures are also clear that God will use the destruction of Mystery Babylon to fulfill many of His purposes in the world:

- God will use the fall of America to bring His people, the Jews, back to Israel:

"The LORD hath brought forth our righteousness: come, and let us declare in Zion the work of the LORD our God."
Jeremiah 51:10

- God's judgment of America will demonstrate His divine attributes: His power, mercy, foresight, and righteousness:

"For true and righteous are his judgments: for he hath judged the great whore, which did corrupt the earth with her fornication, and hath avenged the blood of his servants at her hand."
Revelation 19:2

- God will use the fall of America to raise up a new world power, moving human history closer to its predetermined culmination:

"And I saw a new heaven and a new earth: for the first heaven and the first earth were passed away; and there was no more sea.

And I John saw the holy city, new Jerusalem, coming down from God out of heaven, prepared as a bride adorned for her husband."

Revelation 21:1-2

- God will use the fall of America to warn the nations of a coming future judgment of all the peoples of the earth:

"And I saw the dead, small and great, stand before God; and the books were opened: and another book was opened, which is the book of life: and the dead were judged out of those things which were written in the books, according to their works.

And the sea gave up the dead which were in it; and death and hell delivered up the dead which were in them: and they were judged every man according to their works.

And death and hell were cast into the lake of fire. This is the second death.

And whosoever was not found written in the book of life was cast into the lake of fire."

Revelation 20:12-15

The things which we have discussed are far beyond anything we have ever experienced within our lifetimes thus far. It may be hard to believe these things, but our world is going to change and the current era of relative peace and prosperity will be replaced by ages of increasing war and oppression. God has forewarned us of these things in His Word. Take notice of the signs around you, and turn to God:

"Seek ye the LORD while he may be found, call ye upon him while he is near:

Let the wicked forsake his way, and the unrighteous man his thoughts: and let him return unto the LORD, and he will have mercy upon him; and to our God, for he will abundantly pardon."

Isaiah 55:6-7

Chapter 8:
Is Another American Civil War Possible?

~

"The wicked shall be turned into hell, and all the nations that forget God."
Psalm 9:17

God says there will be another American civil war.

In the last chapter we discussed that the sign God will give to His people that Mystery Babylon (America) is about to be judged will be the beginning of a new civil war in the land:

"And lest your heart faint, and ye fear for the rumour that shall be heard in the land; a rumour shall both come one year, and after that in another year shall come a rumour, and ***violence in the land, ruler against ruler****.*

Therefore, behold, the days come, that I will do judgment upon the graven images of Babylon: and her whole land shall be confounded, and all her slain shall fall in the midst of her."

Jeremiah 51:46-47

This may be a hard thing for many modern Americans to believe, so I would like to dedicate an entire chapter (albeit a short one) to the question "Could there be another American civil war?" If America is truly Mystery Babylon, God says that the answer to that question is yes.

Civil war is not beyond the scope of possibility.

We must not forget that America did already experience the American Civil War, and that conflict is a tremendous part of our national history. Despite the horrors of many modern American conflicts, the American Civil War remains the bloodiest war in American history, in terms of American dead. More Americans died of disease in captivity during the Americal Civil War than the United States lost in the entirety of the Vietnam War. Most Americans on both sides of the Civil War foolishly believed that the conflict would be quickly over in a few months, but a whole host of factors, including new rifles and other military developments as well as incompetence and inefficiency in military leadership, led to the war dragging out for a bitter four years. Both sides lost good men, true American patriots.

The beginning of the American Civil War demonstrates an important point; that very small things can build up to an outcome that no one really wanted even despite the best efforts to prevent that outcome. We see many of the same factors in the antebellum America of the past as we do in modern America: greatly polarized moral and political views, with parties unwilling to bend or compromise, a foolish underestimation of the capabilities and determination of the opposing view, a reckless willingness (amongst certain factions) to permit a difference of views to lead to actual violent conflict. The American Civil War also demonstrates an overlapping of multiple important moral issues which conflicted: slavery and states' rights. Americans readily remember that the American Civil War was fought over the national sin of slavery, but often forget that good men fought against the Federal government on the side of slavery because they believed that since their home states had voted to voluntarily join the United States of America, that these states also had the right to withdraw from the Union at will. These men, including men like Robert E. Lee, felt that their loyalty first came to their home states and not to the Federal government itself.

We see many such seemingly conflicting moral dilemmas in modern America as well. If the Federal government were ever again militarily divided against some American states, good men would choose once again to fight on both sides of the conflict. Many today say that "states don't have rights" (I read this assertion just recently) but this is an oversimplification based on the outcome of the last

American Civil War; a great many American citizens today *still do* believe that states have the right to voluntarily secede from the Union, and there are often circulating rumors of American states or regions considering to do so once again.

Divisions within America contribute to the likelihood of civil war.

The structure of the American system could easily facilitate another civil war. The Federal government is the glue that holds the states together, but as the Federal government becomes more politically divided we have seen the tendency of some parties to attempt to win power in government by any means possible; "hook or crook" I believe is the expression. We saw this during the original Obama election, where the dead came out to vote in record numbers and many people on social media were flouting the fact that they had somehow managed to vote three or four times by various means. The political left has long resisted any attempts to reform the voting process and institute safeguards there, such as new voter identification laws, but this is extremely shortsighted. If America ever reached the point where large portions of the American population felt that the voting process had become compromised, American confidence in the Federal government and office of the Presidency (already low) would evaporate nearly instantaneously. If the Federal government loses legitimacy due to corruption or voting manipulation, the glue that holds the fifty states together will be gone.

And the individual American states are increasingly polarized. I recently read a quite detailed article about the status quo of American politics on the state level across the nation; according to this article, only one state (Minnesota, if I recall correctly) has a bipartisan state government at the present time. According to that article, all other states have either Democratic or Republican majorities in their statehouses, and those parties are utilizing their present political dominance to ramrod as much legislation through as possible while their time lasts. In one state, Colorado, Democratic lawmakers were pushing through so much legislation that Republicans enacted a rule that new legislation had to be read out loud; Democrats responded by having four computers simultaneously read bills at high speeds, an affront which was later deemed to be unconstitutional after a lawsuit. Elected officials are increasingly aggressive and even militant; one Republican congressman made a comment on social media about trillions of bullets being "on our side." There is increasingly a lack of empathy, understanding, and basic courtesy between the political parties.

If any coalition of states turned against the Federal government, or the Federal government collapsed entirely and the states turned against each other, or even if one political party wholesale boycotted the outcome of an election, the situation could very rapidly deteriorate into a very intense, armed, high collateral damage conflict. *Every* American state (and most American territories) has its own National Guard and Air National Guard units, and the total numbers of these forces across the nation is nearly half a million persons. There are also more than 600,000 law enforcement personnel in the United States of America (and rising), and the training, equipment, and tactics of police officers is increasingly militarized as police forces purchase surplus military vehicles and weapons from the United States armed forces. There are nearly one and a half million American active duty military personnel. And there are more firearms in America than there are American citizens: over 300,000,000. These figures mean that in the event of civil conflict within America or between states, individual states will each have their own militaries which (currently) are answerable to the governors of the states. This is a sobering state of affairs to think about in consideration of a potential American civil war.

There are also many political issues which could very easily ignite violence in America. The phrase "from my cold, dead hands" is quite popular within firearms enthusiast communities, referring to gun owners' determination to resist firearms confiscation by the government (also known as "gun grabs"); the right to gun ownership has been a historic pillar of America. Many Democrats have been quite vocal about even going so far as to confiscate firearms from American citizens, but their views are foolish and shortsighted. A large number of Americans see the Constitution as being the highest law of the land, and the Second Amendment to that Constitution grants to the people the right to "keep and bear arms." In a nation where government is "of the People, by the People, for the People," many Americans believe that the People need to be equipped to defend themselves against tyranny, and almost by definition any attempt by government to sieze the People's arms would be itself an act of tyranny. Many Americans remember that the first action of an oppressive regime is often to take away the citizens' ability to protect themselves; British troops attempted to sieze the American colonists' arms at Lexington and Concord, and that attempted siezure sparked what some observers consider to the the first true American civil war: the War of American Independence.

There are alread rumors of another American civil war in the land.

Public opinion feels that another American civil war is possible, if not already impending. A Canadian article asserted what I hinted at in the paragraph above, that America has actually experienced *three* civil wars: the War of American Independence from Great Britain, the American Civil War, and the election of President Trump marks the beginning of the third civil war. The article mentioned that Trump's election represents America's marked departure from the status quo of the two established political parties, which is evidenced by both parties' obvious hatred of the current American President. That article offered an interesting perspective: that the third civil war has begun already, and it will soon become a violent civil war.

Late last year, National Public Radio posted an article titled "Another 'Civil War'? Pessimism About Political Violence Deepens in a Divided Nation," which mentioned several other articles on the subject which were published in *The American Conservative* and *The Federalist*. That article also mentioned a CBS News poll in which 73% of respondents felt that "the tone of political debate" encouraged violence. The *Washington Post* ran an article some months ago entitled "In America, talk turns to something not spoken of for 150 years: Civil war." The topic of civil war has been picked up and discussed much by politicians and academics. In an earlier chapter, I mentioned that another poll suggested that more than a quarter of American voters feel we may have another civil war within five years. While public perception and sentiment are not an infallible indicator of future events, the mindset of the populace can often lead to a self-fulfillment of these perceptions.

Can these things be averted or postponed?

God is merciful, and I do believe that since God has not been specific as to the exact timing of these things, there could be some flexibility in terms of when God's prophecies concerning America's destruction are fulfilled. God has said that Mystery Babylon *will* fall, and this prophecy is sure, so these future events cannot be completely averted indefinitely. In the Scriptures, God often delayed judgment for nations and individuals who repented of their wickedness and turned back to God, such as the great pagan city of Nineveh in the book of Jonah. But I also look at American society and realize that we are moving in the wrong direction; America is embracing sexual perversion, hedonism, and idolatry on a level never before seen in human history. Can America still experience another great national spiritual revival?

I cannot say with certainty, but I know that God does not lie:

"If my people, which are called by my name, shall humble themselves, and pray, and seek my face, and turn from their wicked ways; then will I hear from heaven, and will forgive their sin, and will heal their land."
2 Chronicles 7:14

God weighs all nations in His balance and governs their rise and fall. Abraham intervened for wicked Sodom and Gomorrah, and God agreed to spare them if ten righteous souls could be found within those cities. Abraham might have felt that those cities were secure after his prayers to God, because his nephew Lot and Lot's family lived in Sodom. Abraham may have known some others of God's people living there; Sodom was the "big city" where Abraham's entourage may have occasionally gone to trade. But the cities of the plain fell short in God's estimation and they were judged. God in His mercy sent angels (messengers) to bring Lot and his family out prior to the destruction of those cities by heavenly fire and brimstone (sulphur); the full account can be read in the book of Genesis, chapters 18 and 19.

Likewise God's people living in the United States have been given a clear messenger in God's Word. Let us pray for America, let us do our utmost to bring her back to her godly historic roots, but when the time is come for her judgment, let us leave without looking back. Those things we loved in America were her best virtues, and we will carry them forward with us wherever we go.

"And if thine eye offend thee, pluck it out, and cast it from thee: it is better for thee to enter into life with one eye, rather than having two eyes to be cast into hell fire."
Matthew 18:9

Chapter 9:
How to Prepare for All These Things

~

"And that, knowing the time, that now it is high time to awake out of sleep: for now is our salvation nearer than when we believed.

The night is far spent, the day is at hand: let us therefore cast off the works of darkness, and let us put on the armour of light.

Let us walk honestly, as in the day; not in rioting and drunkenness, not in chambering and wantonness, not in strife and envying.

But put ye on the Lord Jesus Christ, and make not provision for the flesh, to fulfil the lusts thereof."

Romans 13:11-14

Be prepared for the upheaval and chaotic times ahead.

We have discussed some very disturbing things in the pages of this book and in the pages of Scripture. Proverbs 22:3 says that a prudent man foresees evil and hides himself from it, but a fool plunges ahead without looking and falls right into the evil waiting there. If you take God at His Word (as I do), now is the time to prepare for difficult times ahead. The Bible is clear that as history progresses, the world will become more and more broken, hateful, and warlike. There will be great hardships ahead for all peoples.

Therefore I would like to spend a little time to discuss what should be done to safeguard our families and friends for the times ahead. There are a great many common sense measures which can be taken in order to prepare for most situations, whether natural disasters, civil upheaval, widespread power outages, etc. We cannot always blithely assume that the future will be as forgiving to the unprepared as the past has been in this country. Notice that I am just an ordinary fellow; I don't have a well-stocked island paradise somewhere to which I will whisk away when destruction eventually comes to the United States. I will have to do what I can and trust God for the rest, and at the end of the day, this is all that anyone can really do.

Without further ado, let us discuss those things which we can do:

#1 Do not be afraid.

"Fear thou not; for I am with thee: be not dismayed; for I am thy God: I will strengthen thee; yea, I will help thee; yea, I will uphold thee with the right hand of my righteousness."

Isaiah 41:10

God's Word says things like "fear not" and "do not be afraid" dozens upon dozens of times. Why? Even in the midst of violence, upheaval, famine, or impending death, God is still the one and only uncontested ruler of the universe. All things are under His omnipotent control. Jesus Christ told His disciples that God takes notice of every sparrow, and knows even the number of hairs on our heads.

Fear is often a natural side effect of situations which are far beyond our control. We human beings do not like being out of control, but ultimately there are a great many things that we cannot change or influence. Instead of panicking and acting in rash terror, we must trust in God's providential care.

I would be remiss if I didn't mention something quite important. The Bible was written largely for and to God's people, and admonitions to "fear not" are likewise for those Christians who know God. If you do not know Jesus Christ, or if you are actively resisting His Lordship in your life, *there is a great deal to fear.* Earthly troubles are just the tip of the iceberg for you, friend, and beyond them eternal judgment awaits. If you do not know Jesus Christ as your Lord and Savior, I implore you to seek God's face and consider the things I have written at the end of this chapter.

Only God's children can truly live without fear.

#2 Have an exit strategy.

In the case of America's eventual destruction,

there is really only one thing that *must* be done in order to survive: get out. The wise and prudent will see the signs in advance and do what needs to be done to leave the country prior to America's downfall. The less prudent will realize at some point, as the violence of the civil war escalates and the situation looks increasingly desperate, that it is time to make a last minute escape from the United States. The foolish or uninformed will attempt to wait things out, hoping that civil order will be restored eventually.

As the signs become clear, I think the best thing will be to make preparations early. Many Americans make plans to retire abroad where the cost of living is much lower, so their savings will stretch much longer. Look ahead and begin to make arrangements for travel (passports for the family, etc.) and future lodging abroad. Do not panic and "jump the gun" so to speak, but do not procrastinate preparations to the degree that you will be unable to move when necessity demands it.

Where should anyone fleeing America look to go? This is a difficult question, because the effects of America's fall will ripple across the globe, and many other nations will collapse or be destroyed in the aftermath. Choosing a new home country poorly may result in jumping "out of the frying pan, into the fire." I am hardly an expert on this matter, having been outside of the United States only once myself, but I will say that the Scriptures strongly point God's people towards Israel in the passages we have studied concerning the fall of Mystery Babylon. This would be my own personal first choice.

Fortunately for me, I have had an interest in the Hebrew language for many years, first taking a class at university and then continuing some basic study by myself. Many Americans looking to relocate would likely prefer to emigrate to a nation where English is the main language; this may or may not be a wise choice, and I would recommend that anyone with an interest in language should study a second language just in case. English is (fortunately for us Americans) already the primary world language of commerce, but being able to converse with more people will open more doors of opportunity. Knowing Spanish will make most of South America more accessible, and a great many Americans retire to Ecuador and other South American nations. Anyone can learn another language efficiently and economically through a variety of free resources,
such as the excellent Duolingo application which I currenly use as one tool for learning Hebrew.

Financial assets will need to be protected and made available for a relocation to another country as well. The most stereotypical method for doing this would be to open a Swiss bank account (or any prudently chosen foreign bank). Remember that any savings in American currencies or securities will likely be worthless without an actual America to vouchsafe them. Gold is typically a pretty universal store of wealth; perhaps Russian currency might be a good investment choice also. I really am no expert here, either; it is difficult to say which nations will still be stable (financially or otherwise) after the United States is removed from the international system. It is rumored that a great many nations (China was the most recent that I read about) are buying large amounts of gold; having such assets on hand means a nation could potentially be more economically stable in case the international finance system collapses.

#3 Store necessities like food, water, and medical supplies.

Do not expect to rely on help from the government or others when America's troubles come. The police will be occupied when America's end is looming. The military will have no idea what to do. The masses will be overtaken by terror. Most will be unable to help themselves and will not survive God's judgment of Mystery Babylon.

Most Americans are gravely unprepared for even the most ordinary disasters which affect this country on an ordinary basis: hurricanes, tornados, power outages, violent crime, etc. Only a tiny percentage of Americans have enough potable water and food on hand to last even a couple weeks in the event of a disaster.

In the case of God's destruction of America, we already mentioned that getting out is really the only way to have a chance of survival, but it is still wise to have resources stockpiled for the more ordinary disasters that could befall society or your region of the country. Bottled water (the large drums) can be purchased fairly cheaply and you should keep enough on hand for several weeks of usage by your family in case of a long-term power outage. If you can afford it, having more set aside is better; you may be able to be a blessing to your extended family, friends, and neighbors if you have a surplus. Likewise you should have some nonperishable foods set aside for emergencies; check on these periodically though because even things like survival rations do not taste particularly good after five years, or may spoil (I speak from personal experience).

Having extra fuel on hand for vehicles could also be important depending on your particular situation and the particular emergency. It is a good idea to have a couple gas cans "just in case" full of stabilized fuel or (preferably) ethanol-free fuel for long-term storage. Owning a small gasoline generator can keep various appliances going when the electricity goes out. There is a great deal more that could be said about emergency preparedness, but that is not ultimately the purpose of this book, so I will stop here with just these basic notes. Other books and resources can help you and your family to be prepared for a truly serious emergency situation. The important thing to keep in mind is that in a truly dire emergency, you and your family may be forced to rely on yourselves for the basic necessities of life and for protection.

#4 Make others aware that America's judgment is coming.

Think of all the friends, family, and acquaintances that you know in your life; how terrible if you could give them a warning to save themselves, but neglect to do so! By the time the impending destruction is apparent to all, it may be far too late for them to be able to run. The Bible verse just inside the cover of this book was a tremendous challenge to me as I wrestled with the question of whether to write this book at all. I believe God's Word to be true and infallible; I believe that the Bible is quite clear about America's identity as Mystery Babylon. I take God at His Word when He vowed to judge Mystery Babylon for her wickedness. For these reasons, I could not in good conscience *not* write this book. I am willing to sacrifice my social reputation in order to broadcast these things to anyone who will listen.

And who knows? There is great blessing in giving to others and in sharing truth, but sometimes we are blessed when they, in turn, give back to us. Perhaps those we warn about perils ahead will one day come to our rescue when we need it.

#5 Believe on the Lord Jesus Christ and you will be saved.

The judgment which is coming to America will be horrific. If it happens within my lifetime, and I hope that it will not, I fully expect that it will overshadow me for the rest of my life, should I survive it. But Mystery Babylon's judgment is just the merest foretaste of a much more personal judgment that every human being will one day experience if they die in their sins without knowing Jesus Christ as Lord and Savior.

You see, the Bible tells us that every human being alive is broken; the Bible calls this brokenness *sin;* sin is the breaking of God's laws. I am sure you have heard of God's Ten Commandments, listed in Exodus chapter 20:

- *"Thou shalt not have any other gods before Me."*
- *"Thou shalt not make unto thee any graven image... thou shalt not bow down thyself to them, nor serve them."*
- *"Thou shalt not take the Name of the Lord thy God in vain."*
- *"Remember the Sabbath day, to keep it holy."*
- *"Honour thy father and thy mother."*
- *"Thou shalt not kill."*
- *"Thou shalt not commit adultery."*
- *"Thou shalt not steal."*
- *"Thou shalt not bear false witness."*
- *"Thou shalt not covet."*
  Exodus 20:3-17

Think about how much better life would be if

everyone always followed God's laws! But the Bible makes it clear that no one has kept God's law perfectly:

"As it is written, There is none righteous, no, not one:

There is none that understandeth, there is none that seeketh after God.

They are all gone out of the way, they are together become unprofitable; there is none that doeth good, no, not one."

Romans 3:10-12

Jesus Christ made it plain why all human beings are unrighteous; even keeping God's law perfectly would not make a person righteous. The human tendency toward wickedness leads us to violate God's law constantly, even in our own minds:

"Ye have heard that it was said by them of old time, Thou shalt not commit adultery:

But I say unto you, That whosoever looketh on a woman to lust after her hath committed adultery with her already in his heart."

Matthew 5:27-28

God, who sees the heart, also sees all the wickedness taking place in the heart, even when we do not act upon those wicked thoughts. Because God is perfectly holy, He cannot tolerate our sin, nor can He excuse it. The penalty for sin is death, both the physical death that we will all one day experience, and a second death: separation from God forever in a terrible place of torment called Hell:

"For the wages of sin is death; but the gift of God is eternal life through Jesus Christ our Lord."
Romans 6:23

"But the fearful, and unbelieving, and the abominable, and murderers, and whoremongers, and sorcerers, and idolaters, and all liars, shall have their part in the lake which burneth with fire and brimstone: which is the second death."
Revelation 21:8

Hell is a very real place; Jesus Christ spoke about it more than He spoke about Heaven. Fallen humanity is on its way to Hell by default; our wickedness separates us from God and earns us the wages, or appropriate payment, for our crimes, which is death. This is a bleak spiritual state in which to be. But here is the good news, the Gospel of Jesus Christ:

"But God commendeth his love toward us, in that, while we were yet sinners, Christ died for us.
Much more then, being now justified by his blood, we shall be saved from wrath through him."
Romans 5:8-9

What does this mean? The Bible is clear that no human sinner can make himself righteous, and if human beings' very thoughts are wicked, how can we be cleansed from sin? It is not something that we can do for ourselves, though many religions falsely teach that people can earn salvation from judgment by doing good works. But good works do not erase sins. Romans 5:8-9 shows that God chose to have mercy upon us even while we were sinners, and sent His Son, Jesus Christ, to earth. Jesus, being God in human form, was able to live a perfect life in accordance with the laws of God. Jesus' sacrifice of His own life on the Cross of Calvary was a sacrifice made in atonement for the sins of wicked humanity. He experienced death in our place so that we would not have to. As Romans 5:9 says, we can be saved from the wrath of God's righteous judgment for our sins because Jesus Christ took that wrath upon Himself.

John 3:16 is the most famous and well-known verse in the Bible:

"For God so loved the world, that he gave his only begotten Son, that whosoever believeth in him should not perish, but have everlasting life."
John 3:16

This is the message of the Gospel, which is the very core of the Bible. This is why God revealed Himself to humanity: to save sinful mankind from sin and a purposeless existence apart from God. Those who accept Jesus Christ as Lord and Savior will never experience the second death in the Lake of Fire forever; they will be joined with Jesus Christ and the saints in eternity. This salvation is a free gift from

God, and cannot be earned or extorted from Him:

"For by grace are ye saved through faith; and that not of yourselves: it is the gift of God:
Not of works, lest any man should boast."
Ephesians 2:8-9

Freed from the threat of future judgment for sins, the spiritual security that the Christian has through Jesus Christ is greater than any physical security a person might have in their short life on earth. Indeed, physical security in this life is so often an illusion. For the Christian, this life and planet are not where we truly live; an eternal home with God will be our final destiny. I hope, friend, that I will see you there someday in the Kingdom of God which will stand forever.

"And Jesus came and spake unto them, saying, All power is given unto me in heaven and in earth.
Go ye therefore, and teach all nations, baptizing them in the name of the Father, and of the Son, and of the Holy Ghost:
Teaching them to observe all things whatsoever I have commanded you: and, lo, I am with you alway, even unto the end of the world. Amen."
Matthew 28:18-20

"Have I any pleasure at all that the wicked should die? saith the Lord GOD: and not that he should return from his ways, and live?"

Ezekiel 18:23

Made in the USA
Middletown, DE
02 July 2019